Cults

OTHER BOOKS OF RELATED INTEREST

Cults

Jill Karson, *Book Editor*

David L. Bender, *Publisher*
Bruno Leone, *Executive Editor*
Bonnie Szumski, *Editorial Director*
David M. Haugen, *Managing Editor*
Brenda Stalcup, *Series Editor*

Contemporary Issues
Companion

Greenhaven Press, Inc., San Diego, CA

Library of Congress Cataloging-in-Publication Data

Cults / Jill Karson, book editor.
        p.   cm. — (Contemporary issues companion)
     Includes bibliographical references (p.   ) and index.
     ISBN 0-7377-0162-5 (pbk. : alk. paper). —
  ISBN 0-7377-0163-3 (lib. bdg. : alk. paper)
     1. Cults I. Karson, Jill. II. Series.
  BP603.C84 2000
  291—dc21   99-20382
                                                                    CIP

©2000 by Greenhaven Press, Inc.
P.O. Box 289009, San Diego, CA 92198-9009

Printed in the U.S.A.

CONTENTS

FOREWORD

In the news, on the streets, and in neighborhoods, individuals are confronted with a variety of social problems. Such problems may affect people directly: A young woman may struggle with depression, suspect a friend of having bulimia, or watch a loved one battle cancer. And even the issues that do not directly affect her private life—such as religious cults, domestic violence, or legalized gambling—still impact the larger society in which she lives. Discovering and analyzing the complexities of issues that encompass communal and societal realms as well as the world of personal experience is a valuable educational goal in the modern world.

Effectively addressing social problems requires familiarity with a constantly changing stream of data. Becoming well informed about today's controversies is an intricate process that often involves reading myriad primary and secondary sources, analyzing political debates, weighing various experts' opinions—even listening to first-hand accounts of those directly affected by the issue. For students and general observers, this can be a daunting task because of the sheer volume of information available in books, periodicals, on the evening news, and on the Internet. Researching the consequences of legalized gambling, for example, might entail sifting through congressional testimony on gambling's societal effects, examining private studies on Indian gaming, perusing numerous websites devoted to Internet betting, and reading essays written by lottery winners as well as interviews with recovering compulsive gamblers. Obtaining valuable information can be time-consuming—since it often requires researchers to pore over numerous documents and commentaries before discovering a source relevant to their particular investigation.

Greenhaven's Contemporary Issues Companion series seeks to assist this process of research by providing readers with useful and pertinent information about today's complex issues. Each volume in this anthology series focuses on a topic of current interest, presenting informative and thought-provoking selections written from a wide variety of viewpoints. The readings selected by the editors include such diverse sources as personal accounts and case studies, pertinent factual and statistical articles, and relevant commentaries and overviews. This diversity of sources and views, found in every Contemporary Issues Companion, offers readers a broad perspective in one convenient volume.

In addition, each title in the Contemporary Issues Companion series is designed especially for young adults. The selections included in every volume are chosen for their accessibility and are expertly edited in consideration of both the reading and comprehension levels of the audience. The structure of the anthologies also enhances accessibility. An introductory essay places each issue in context and provides helpful facts such as historical background or current statistics and legislation that pertain to the topic. The chapters that follow organize the material and focus on specific aspects of the book's topic. Every essay is introduced by a brief summary of its main points and biographical information about the author. These summaries aid in comprehension and can also serve to direct readers to material of immediate interest and need. Finally, a comprehensive index allows readers to efficiently scan and locate content.

The Contemporary Issues Companion series is an ideal launching point for research on a particular topic. Each anthology in the series is composed of readings taken from an extensive gamut of resources, including periodicals, newspapers, books, government documents, the publications of private and public organizations, and Internet websites. In these volumes, readers will find factual support suitable for use in reports, debates, speeches, and research papers. The anthologies also facilitate further research, featuring a book and periodical bibliography and a list of organizations to contact for additional information.

A perfect resource for both students and the general reader, Greenhaven's Contemporary Issues Companion series is sure to be a valued source of current, readable information on social problems that interest young adults. It is the editors' hope that readers will find the Contemporary Issues Companion series useful as a starting point to formulate their own opinions about and answers to the complex issues of the present day.

INTRODUCTION

The images broadcast into homes across America in May 1997 were chilling. Thirty-nine members of the Heaven's Gate cult lay dead in their bunk beds, clad in identical, asexual clothing and covered in purple, diamond-shaped death shrouds. Their suicide was painstakingly orchestrated: The eighteen men and twenty-one women bade farewell to a video camera, packed their belongings, and then killed themselves in shifts, ingesting phenobarbital-laced applesauce and alcohol. According to the videotapes and other materials left behind by the group, the members of Heaven's Gate believed that by shedding their "containers," their spirits would become free to ascend to a higher plane of existence, which they would reach aboard an alien spacecraft that trailed the Hale-Bopp comet.

Although groups like Heaven's Gate are certainly not a new phenomenon, cults are still little understood. Moreover, the occurrence of lurid dramas involving cults—such as the mass suicide of members of Heaven's Gate—raises troublesome questions about cultic ideals, beliefs, and practices.

The word "cult" generally refers to a religious group that holds beliefs that diverge from mainstream religions. A cult may have its roots in established religions such as Christianity or Buddhism, but parts of its doctrine vary significantly from that of the parent religion. Furthermore, cults are typically described as sharing certain traits, including a rigid, authoritarian power structure and a charismatic leader who followers believe is godlike or endowed with ultimate wisdom. This leader may use unethical recruiting tactics to boost cult membership. Followers may be deprived of basic freedoms. The cult's ties to mainstream culture may be weak or completely severed, and the cult may endorse atypical practices such as group marriage or the stockpiling of weapons in anticipation of the end of the world.

However, whether a particular religious group should be considered a cult is not always an easy question to answer. For instance, some commentators consider Jehovah's Witnesses to be a cult because of the strict rules placed on members, such as the requirement that followers must sacrifice many hours each week distributing the group's literature and trying to convert nonmembers. However, other commentators argue that recruitment and similar aspects of Jehovah's Witnesses are also found in some established churches or other groups regarded as valid religions, so these characteristics do not make Jehovah's Witnesses a cult. Estimates of the number of cults in existence therefore vary widely depending on which group or individual is doing the counting. The staunchly anticult American Family Foundation, for example, concludes that there are between three thousand and five thousand active cults in the United States, with between 3 million and 5 million members. Other cult experts, including J. Gordon Melton, find such claims vastly inflated. Melton offers a far more conservative estimate, counting between five and six hundred cultic groups in existence in the United States. To make matters even more confusing, the cult phenomenon is not exclusive to America. Many U.S.-based groups have members in other countries. Jehovah's Witnesses, for example, claim to have hundreds of thousands of members overseas. Other groups that originated outside the United States also have international membership. For instance, Canada's Order of the Solar Temple, while never gaining a large U.S. following, has spread to Switzerland and France. The fact that many cults have an international following makes it even more difficult to determine an accurate count of the number of cultic groups.

Not only do experts disagree over which groups should be considered cults, but they also differ over the use of the term "cult" to describe such organizations. "Cult" is derived from the Latin word "cultus," which simply means a group of people who are devoted to a person or idea. However, the modern usage of the word has gained additional connotations, many of which are negative or derogatory. Cults are often seen as dangerous institutions that threaten the well-being of the individual followers and perhaps also society at large. As Joseph Sobran writes in the *Wanderer*, "Religious cults are getting a bad name. In fact, to call a group a 'cult' is already to condemn it, or at least to raise suspicion and prejudice against it." Thus, to avoid the pejorative connotation of the word "cult," many people choose to employ more neutral terms in describing cultic groups, such as nonmainstream, marginal, alternative, or new religious groups or movements.

The disagreement over the use of the term "cult" is related to another controversy: whether all cultic groups deserve the negative connotations surrounding the word. Critics of cults feel that these organizations have earned their negative reputation. They warn that cults, in contrast to bona fide religions, are extreme groups that stretch the boundaries of ethical behavior. Cults can be distinguished from religions, these critics assert, because they use extreme levels of manipulation and deception to recruit members and then induce complete dependency—convincing followers to sever ties with their families or to turn over their worldly possessions, for example. As cult researcher Willa Appel puts it:

> There is a large store of horror stories about life in the cults—about rape, sexual humiliation, starvation, child abuse, beatings, forced labor, unattended physical illness, and personal degradation. Evidence abounds that these stories . . . are not mere inventions.

In the view of Appel and other experts, tragedies such as the Heaven's Gate collective suicide are directly due to the typical dynamics of a cultic group. They maintain that the power structures, deceptive behaviors, and unusual beliefs found in cultic groups lead to illegal, unethical, and abusive conduct.

According to others, however, cults are not necessarily as bad as critics have maintained, and some cultic groups are completely harmless. While these experts acknowledge that dangerous cults exist, they contend that such groups are the exception rather than the rule. Status as a cult does not necessarily mean that a group is indulging in harmful activities or mistreating members, they assert. Indeed, these commentators point out, many of the world's major religions were considered to be cults in their infancy. For instance, they argue, when Christianity arose, its tenets seemed bizarre or blasphemous to practitioners of more established religions such as Judaism, and early adherents to Christianity were harshly persecuted for their beliefs. As religious historian Lawrence Foster states, "One person's cult is another person's true faith." Since the line between a cult and a religion is fuzzy and not well defined, these experts insist, people should be less hasty to condemn all new religious groups as destructive or harmful.

Many of these commentators also maintain that cults deserve the same religious freedom and protection enjoyed by mainstream religions. A few well-publicized instances of tragic events related to cults have caused all cultic groups and alternative religions to become suspect, they assert, but most groups have done nothing to deserve the negative stigma and persecution they face. Pico Iyer is among those who question the denial of religious freedom to cultic groups, asking, "Who is to determine when a 'cult' becomes a religion, especially in a land where freedom of religion is sacrosanct?" According to Iyer and other commentators, cults have a right to exist without interference, even if their methods or practices diverge from the mainstream.

How to address the issue of cults will only gain urgency, as the number of cults both in the United States and worldwide continues to increase. Since the 1960s, there has been an explosion of new and diverse cultic groups. Some of the more prominent groups include Scientology, the Unification Church, Syanon, Krishna Consciousness, and the Children of God. The nineties, too, beget a new generation of cults, including a variety of New Age groups. Perhaps most significantly, the approach of the year 2000 produced a variety of doomsday cults, including apocalyptic and millennium cults.

Experts hypothesize that new cultic groups will continue to grow in number, with members spread across the globe. Concurrent with this trend, critics of cults are likely to increase their scrutiny in efforts to curb what they regard as dangerous behavior. In such a climate, the questions and issues surrounding cults are important to consider. *Cults: Contemporary Issues Companion* offers a broad perspective for examining the nature of cults and the controversies surrounding their beliefs, practices, and right to exist.

CHAPTER 1

WHAT ARE CULTS?

CULTS: AN OVERVIEW

John A. Saliba

In his study of cults, religious scholar John A. Saliba analyzes the characteristics typically associated with cults (or new religious movements, as he prefers to call them). In addition to listing the negative attributes of cultic groups, Saliba presents some of the positive features that draw people to the new religions, including the intoxicating enthusiasm exhibited by members and the promise of lofty spiritual experiences. While the author does not deny that the demands of some cultic groups are restrictive and possibly even abusive, he is wary of those who indiscriminately apply unfavorable attributes to all cultic groups. Saliba has written extensively on new religions. His books include *Religious Cults Today: A Challenge to Christian Families* and *Understanding New Religious Movements,* from which the following selection is excerpted.

Both scholarly and popular literature is replete with descriptions of the main qualities which enable one to discriminate between cults and the mainline religious organizations. Many of these characteristics are related to the definition of a cult. Two diverse schools of thought can be found in contemporary literature. Both need to be considered since their respective views have been debated in society at large and in the law courts. One tends to take a rather negative approach and lists the pejorative qualities of cult ideology and lifestyle. The other adopts a somewhat neutral or cautionary optimistic perspective which concedes that there are good features in the new religious movements, features which may outweigh, in the long run, the defective elements in their beliefs and practices and offer an explanation of why people get involved in them. The major problem with these attempts to depict cults is that new religions do not form one amorphous body with exactly the same characteristics. They do, however, share some traits and can thus be grouped together under one name.

Adapted excerpt from John A. Saliba, *Understanding New Religious Movements,* ©1995 by John Saliba, Wm. B. Eerdmans Publishing Co., Grand Rapids, Michigan, USA. Used by permission of the publisher.

Negative Features

A widely accepted representative model that lists schematically the unfavorable qualities of the cults is provided by James and Marcia Rudin, authors of *Prison or Paradise: The New Religious Cults*, who represent the opinion of those who consider practically all new religious groups as dangerous institutions that threaten the individual's mental and physical health, the family's well-being, and the established cultural traditions as a whole. The Rudins list fourteen attributes of the new cults which can be summarized as follows:

(1) the swearing of total allegiance to an all-powerful leader, believed to be the Messiah;
(2) the discouragement of rational thought;
(3) often-deceptive recruitment techniques;
(4) a weakening of the members' psychological make-up;
(5) the manipulation of guilt;
(6) isolation from the outside world;
(7) complete power of the leader, who decides whatever the members do;
(8) dedication of all energy and finances to the cult, or sometimes, to the benefit of the leader;
(9) cult members work full-time for the group without adequate pay;
(10) cults are anti-women, anti-child, or even anti-family;
(11) belief that the end of the world is near at hand;
(12) an ethical system that adopts the principle that the end justifies the means;
(13) an aura of secrecy and mystery;
(14) frequently, an aura of violence or potential violence.

These features, taken together, furnish an overwhelming and frightening image of a cult. Though the authors are careful to inform their readers that their comprehensive list of features is a generalization, the overall impression one gets is that they are typical and that many of them are found in most of the new religions. It would be difficult, if not impossible, however, to find a single new religious movement to which even a few of the above attributes are applicable. Some of the listed traits (such as the discouragement of rational thought) can be easily misunderstood or taken out of context. Others (such as the requirement that members work full-time without pay) could be also ascribed to some of the mainline religions, more particularly to monastic institutions in both the Christian and Buddhist traditions. The following reflections on three of the more commonly mentioned negative characteristics are intended to show that the prevalent image of a new religion, which the Rudins outline so graphically, is somewhat imprecise, misleading, and incorrect.

The first feature listed by the Rudins, which seems to allude to a ritual act in which total allegiance is sworn to a leader, can be misunderstood if considered without reference to the ideology that demands total obedience to religious founders. That some cult leaders have final authority over their disciples in both spiritual and material matters is certainly the case. These leaders are at times believed to be inspired by God, from whom they receive special revelations and instructions. Or again, as in the case with many sectarian gurus of Indian origin, they are accepted as representatives of God and are obeyed accordingly. Benjamin Walker, in his encyclopedia of Hinduism, writes that

> the living guru is believed to be the embodiment of the founder-deity and he is thus the last in line of succession starting from the god. As he is the deity incarnate, salvation is possible through him alone. . . . Frequently the living guru himself is actually worshiped.

The sacred literature of several new religions includes, besides the Bible, an additional book the contents of which are believed to be revealed or inspired. The *Divine Principle* of the Unification Church is an excellent example. Other new religions rely on the writings and lectures of their leaders for providing the best guidance for reaching the goals proposed by the movement. The writings of Ron Hubbard, the (deceased) founder of the Church of Scientology, are a case in point.

The leaders of those groups, who are held to be in touch with superior beings from other planes or with the 'Ascended Masters', as is the case with Elizabeth Clare Prophet of the Church Universal and Triumphant (Summit Lighthouse), exercise religious authority over their followers. Not many of the new movements maintain that their leaders or prophets are the Messiah in the Christian meaning of the term. What members of new religions do is similar to what all religious believers do, that is, they locate the basis for religious authority, the acceptance of which, as in all religious traditions, depends ultimately on a faith commitment and not on indisputable, logical deduction or empirical evidence.

There are definitely gurus who have misused their authority, cult leaders who are pompous, self-righteous individuals, and spiritual leaders who have over-inflated egos. Being a great charismatic personality does not automatically imply holiness or even good ethical conduct as disclosures about television evangelists in the 1980s have demonstrated. But it would be unrealistic to make the blanket statement that all the leaders of new religious movements are corrupt, pseudoreligious prophets who are mainly interested in financial gain and power, just as it would be unfair to call all politicians crooks and all evangelical preachers hypocrites.

Cults as Proselytizing Religious Groups

Another of those features that are constantly mentioned in the context of new religious movements is their high-handed evangelism or proselytization. Cult members are seen as enthusiastic followers of a particular charismatic leader or as fanatical preachers of a particular belief, like the imminent coming of the end of the world. To many members of the mainline (non-evangelical) churches they appear too zealous in sharing their spiritual experiences, too intent on advertising their religious beliefs, and a little too forceful in their efforts to recruit people to their worldviews, lifestyles, and plans for a better society.

Images of such missionary endeavors are plentiful and tend to persist even when the cults change or abandon them. Members of the Hare Krishna Movement are remembered for their dancing at major street corners, for talking to people about the joys and benefits of chanting their mantra, and for accosting travelers at airports to hand out their colorful literature for a donation. Again, one can mention the evangelizing techniques of the Unification Church on college campuses where students are accosted and invited to a dinner at the house shared by several members. In the early 1970s the Jesus People frequently stole the headlines by their bold street ministry that included accosting people and asking them whether they had been saved. Some will also vividly recall those occasions when they were the object of evangelical activities of older and more established religious groups. The Mormons still have their young adults embark on missionary programs which include visiting people in their homes, talking to them about religious matters pertinent to Mormonism, and distributing their literature. Many churchgoers, returning to their parked cars after Sunday worship, have found propaganda literature of the Seventh-Day Adventists attached to the windshields of their cars. Members of new religions seem very active in disseminating their spiritual knowledge and recounting the experiences that led them to their new commitments or confirmed them in their religious beliefs.

When one reflects, however, on the number and variety of new religious organizations in the West, the vision of a cult as, essentially, a forceful evangelistic group begins to fade. In the Western world there are probably several hundred religious groups which have been labeled 'cults'. Of these, the number of controversial ones—those that have stirred up public concern and antagonistic reactions—number around fifty. When one tries to enumerate those groups that employ forceful proselytization methods one is apt to come up with a very short list. The majority of new religions do not advertise in public but keep a rather low profile; neither do they have their members at street corners selling flowers or on college and university campuses discussing philosophical issues; nor do they send missionaries from door to door. Those that make active recruiting a major portion of their daily activities are the exceptions, not the rule. There are, for instance, many Buddhist groups that do not engage in heavy propaganda. It is thus possible that many people have become members of new religions because they discovered on their own the group they joined, rather than because they were actually sought after and successfully recruited by pushy devotees.

Linked to the idea that members of all cults are heavy proselytizers is the assertion that they consciously employ deceptive techniques to lure people to join them. This is probably one of the more serious attacks against the cults. But, once again, it would be difficult to substantiate this charge against the new religious movements in general and, thus, unrealistic to enumerate deception as one of their main features. In fact the two most-quoted examples of deceptive evangelization methods are the recruitment practices of the Unification Church and of the now defunct People's Temple.

Deceptive recruiting practices, when and if they occur, might present societal problems and ways should be devised to cope with them. But the customary accusation that members of new religions intentionally use deception could stem from misunderstanding and/or overgeneralization. In many cases involving groups who recruit openly, deception is hardly possible. The devotees of the Hare Krishna Movement, dancing and singing their mantra at a street corner or in front of a large department store, couldn't possibly be intentionally disguising their identity. Their literature could hardly be mistaken for Gospel tracts. Similarly, a visit to a Zen temple cannot lead even the casual visitor to conclude that he or she has just been given a tour of a Christian monastery.

Cults as Rigid, All-Embracing Institutions

A third image of a cult is that of an organization that has tight control of its members who live in communes or closely knit communities. Several cults certainly fit into this pattern. Those members of the Hare Krishna Movement who do not marry, the 'sannyasin', live a monastic lifestyle. In New Vrindaban, a relatively large splinter branch of the Hare Krishna Movement in West Virginia, all members—some married, others not—live in a commune-style environment with many daily activities, like meals, shared in common. The Unification Church and several Yoga groups have community dwellings or ashrams, even though the number of individuals living communally represents a small percentage of the membership.

Not all new religions, however, have communal living as a requirement for membership. Most of the members of, for example, Scientology, Transcendental Meditation, several Christian fundamentalist groups, and occult organizations do not live in communal settings. Even among those who encourage community living, varieties of lifestyles are allowed. Not all members of the Hare Krishna Movement are expected to live a monastic life and not all members of the Church Universal and Triumphant share commune-style ranches. Once again, the popular image of the cult as a tight monastic institution does not always conform with the facts.

Another reason why the cults have been accused of applying a rigid socialization process to maintain their members is that they seem so dogmatic in their teachings. Members of new religious movements claim that they have found answers to all their religious questions and mundane problems. In a changing, complex world where religious pluralism is rampant, one wonders how people can be so absolute in their views and so intolerant of diverse opinions. Individuals are drawn to particular alternative religions because their members appear happy in their living arrangements, satisfied with their involvement, and able to speak about their commitment with certainty. One must further bear in mind that committed members do not usually find this disciplined religious doctrine restrictive; to them it is rather conducive to the spiritual goals they hope to attain.

Another critique of the activities of founders of new religions is that they demand their members to dedicate a lot of time to the spread of the movement's ideology. Further, they regulate and control the daily lives of the devotees and, in some cases, also dictate how members should relate to one another and to the outside world. The fixed marriages of the Unification Church are a typical example. Such customs appear to be directly opposed to the Western stress on individual freedom.

It is possible, however, that the control which leaders of new religions have over their members should be seen as a manifestation of intense commitment and dedication. Some new religions can be better understood in the light of the sociological concept of 'total institution'. Samuel Wallace writes in *Total Institutions*:

> When any type of social institution—religious, educational, legal or medical—begins to exercise total control over its population, that institution begins to display certain characteristics: communication between insider and outsider is rigidly controlled or prohibited altogether; those inside the institution are frequently referred to as inmates—subjects whose every movement is controlled by the institution's staff; an entirely separate social world comes into existence within the institution, which defines the inmate's social status, his relationship to all others, his very identity as a person.

Erving Goffman, who has written at length about the restrictions of total institutions, lists five types of such groups, the last being:

> those establishments designed as retreats from the world even while often serving as training centers for the religious; examples are abbeys, monasteries, convents, and other cloisters.

Attractive Features

One must, consequently, be wary of writers who draw up elaborate lists of unfavorable characteristics that are indiscriminately applied to

all new religions. Several of the features listed above, like proselytization and dogmatism, can possibly be applied also to traditional religions or churches. One should be even more suspicious of those who
seem to detect nothing else in the new religions but negative elements and nefarious intentions on the part of leaders and recruiters.

One of the main problems which the listing of negative features of
cults has is that it makes it extremely difficult to explain why young
adults would even consider joining them. There must be appealing
qualities that draw people to the fringe religions. It is precisely these
qualities that one must know if one is to understand the reasons for
their success and to respond appropriately. The selected characteristics
listed below are general and refer to those qualities that are both
sought by would-be members and promised by the new religions
themselves. The fact that a large percentage of those who join new
religions leave after a year or two suggests that these religions do not
always deliver what they promote and leave many of their members
disappointed. It should also be emphatically stated that even obviously attractive features are not necessarily an unmixed blessing.

Great Enthusiasm

Probably one of the more obvious features in most, if not all, members
of new religious movements is their enthusiasm for the new faith they
have discovered and the lifestyle they have embraced. Enthusiasm
may not always translate itself into great missionary fervor and prose-
lytizing activities, but its presence is strongly felt. Gatherings of members at which guests are invited may include testimonies that relate
the great benefits of membership. Stories of personal conversion, typical also of evangelical and Pentecostal Christianity, have an appealing
and almost irresistible quality. They tend to leave a strong impression
that members are passionately involved in a worthwhile cause and
have found the peace and security that so many people desire.

Underlying this enthusiasm is the dedication and commitment
which members so openly exhibit. To people who are nominal members of the church of their upbringing, the intense dedication and
unqualified commitment of their relatives and friends to a marginal
religious group can be both bewildering and threatening. To those
dissatisfied with their current religious orientation the beliefs and
practices of new religious movements might appear both challenging
and promising. And to young adults who are concerned about the
lack of religiousness in contemporary Western culture, life in a new
religion may seem to offer a haven from a society that stresses utilitar-
ian, materialistic, and self-gratifying values and downgrades those
higher aspirations normally linked with religion.

Religious enthusiasm, of course, is not a characteristic found only
in members of new religious movements. Despite its appeal, enthusiasm could, if unchecked, degenerate into fanaticism and lead to ten-

sions and conflicts between religious groups. In their enthusiastic campaigns to enlist new members, some of the new movements have been rightly accused of making themselves public nuisances, failing to respect the sensitivities of others, and unjustly criticizing the works and achievements of traditional churches. When condemning the recruitment techniques used by new religions, it would be wise to bear in mind that many of their methods are hardly original and have, at times, been deployed by Christian evangelists and missionaries.

Stress on Experience

Another notable, though by no means unique, characteristic of the new movements is their stress on experience. They offer not just different creeds, moralities, and lifestyles, but also new spiritual experiences. Members of new religions, like evangelical Christians, talk about the 'unique' religious feeling they have come in touch with since their conversion. Whether it be speaking in tongues, or the practice of meditation, or the recitation of a mantra, or contact with the guru, the message is the same. The individual claims that he or she has been transformed by the experience. This explains, in part, why it is difficult to convince members of new religions that they have chosen a wrong path.

Central to religious life in all traditions is the experience of the holy. Such an experience, however, can be deceptive or hallucinatory. Some drugs can, apparently, create spiritual and mystical experiences, especially the feeling of being one with God and/or of having achieved cosmic consciousness. Scholars have explored the possible similarity between the 'mystical' experiences of Christian saints and the altered states of consciousness or peak experiences of those who have experimented with mind-altering drugs. Many conversion experiences reported by members of new religious movements have been likened to the effects of the drug LSD. In the earlier years of the Jesus Movement young adults were encouraged to abandon their counterculture lifestyle and to accept and experience Jesus. They claimed that they were 'high' on Jesus, an obvious reference to the drug experiences that they had before their conversions.

It is understandable that the promise of a deep, lasting religious or spiritual experience is alluring. The evaluation of such experiences is, however, far from easy. There are no universally accepted criteria for determining the validity and authenticity of a spiritual experience. The suggestion that experiences require critical reflection and need to be balanced by reason may, in fact, be rejected by many converts both to new and more traditional religions. Even if one adopts a definite theological opinion on the nature of religious experience, conversions to the new religions cannot be simply dismissed as spurious. The new religions tend to idealize, channel, and control specific experiences, but they do not, as a rule, discourage or stifle self-reflection, as is so commonly thought.

The Practice of Spiritual Disciplines

New religions do not necessarily succeed in attracting members because they present overwhelming theological systems and irresistible philosophical arguments or because they have achieved their goals of creating ideal communal-living arrangements. Converts talk about the personal benefits of membership. The cure of personal ills, the resolution of individual problems, and the improvement in their mental and psychological well-being are at times advertised as the advantages of becoming a member of a new religion. The practice of meditation or contemplation is a good example of a remedy offered by some of the new religions. Practitioners of Transcendental Meditation, for instance, have dedicated a lot of effort to convince people that the daily, structured recitation of the personal mantra, given individually to each initiated member, leads to physical, emotional, intellectual, and spiritual improvement and promotes a better social existence. Meditation, it is argued, has a calming, beneficial effect on the human body and mind and on the personality as a whole. In an industrialized society that is characterized by a fast-moving pace that allows little time for solitary self-reflection, that tends to increase anxiety, and that often leads to alienation and depersonalization, the recitation of mantras, or a period of quiet reflection in a yoga posture, could certainly be appealing.

In many of the new religions spiritual practices become part of the daily routine of each member. They may provide a much desired escape from the hectic lifestyle of Western culture. In this respect it is easy to compare them to the prayerful and meditative lifestyles found in more traditional religious institutions, such as Christian and Buddhist monasteries. Once again, however, religious practices and lifestyles require careful scrutiny. Long hours of meditation, ascetical practices, and monastic regimes are not automatically beneficial to everybody. When members of new religious movements ignore medical care and replace it with meditation, faith-sharing sessions, and mantra recital, the concern about their mental and physical health is certainly justifiable.

THE DIFFERENCE BETWEEN HARMFUL AND BENIGN CULTS

James R. Lewis

Despite society's tendency to stigmatize groups with unorthodox religious views, most cults are completely harmless, according to James R. Lewis. In the following essay, Lewis debunks commonly held stereotypes about "dangerous" cults and cult leaders and presents his own criteria for distinguishing potentially harmful groups. For example, he writes, cult observers commonly label any group led by a charismatic leader who asserts divine authority as dangerous. However, according to Lewis, this stereotype is inaccurate; many leaders claim to be prophets or messiahs and yet very few pose any danger to their followers or to society. More meaningful criteria include examining how leaders use their authority to guide followers or how they tolerate dissent within their ranks, he maintains. James Lewis is a religious scholar with a strong background in Hindu-based religious groups. He has written and edited many books and articles on religious topics.

While the majority of minority religions are innocuous, many have been involved in social conflicts. A handful of these conflicts have made national and even international headlines, from the 1993 siege of the Branch Davidian community to the 1997 group suicide of Heaven's Gate members. One consequence of these highly publicized incidents is that they have served to reinforce unreflective stereotypes about "cults" and "cult leaders" that are appropriate for some—but certainly not the majority of—minority religions. Unfortunately, such stereotyped information is often the only "data" readily available to the media and law enforcement at the onset of such conflicts.

Putting aside the technical discourse of sociologists, in ordinary language people talk as if there is an objective category of groups called "cults" that can be distinguished from genuine religions. In this commonly accepted view, cults are by definition socially dangerous false religions, led by cynical cult leaders who exploit followers for their own gain.

Reprinted from James R. Lewis, "Safe Sects? Early Warning Signs of 'Bad Religions,'" www.religioustolerance.org/safe_sec.htm, by permission of the author.

This stereotype is, however, deeply flawed, and for more than one reason. In the first place, "cult" is a socially-negotiated label that often means little more than a religion one dislikes for some reason. To certain conservative Christians, for example, a "cult" is any religion that departs from a certain traditional interpretation of scripture. Alternately, ultra-conservative Christians who take a strictly fundamentalist approach to scripture often appear "cult-like" to many mainline Christians. In other words, one person's cult is another person's religion.

In the second place, the founders of new groups are—despite whatever personal flaws some might have—almost always sincerely religious. Part of the problem here is that most people unreflectively assume that religion is always something "good." If, therefore, a given religious body does something "bad," then ipso facto it must not be "real" religion. Instead, it must be a false religion, created for no other reason than the founder/leader's personal gain. This attitude is, however, naive. The ancient Aztecs, to take an extreme example, regularly tortured and sacrificed other human beings as part of their religious rites. These practices were, in fact, a central aspect of the Aztec religion. But, however much we might be able to explain and even to understand why the Aztecs engaged in such practices, no contemporary person would defend these rites as "good."

Dangerous Groups

The proper question to ask, then, is not whether some particular group is or is not a cult (in the sense of a "false religion"), but, rather, whether or not the social-psychological dynamics within a particular religion are potentially dangerous to its members and/or to the larger society. Unfortunately, once we get beyond such actions as torturing and murdering other human beings, the criteria for what one regards as harmful can be quite subjective. It has been seriously asserted, for example, that requiring "cult" members to be celibate and to follow vegetarian diets are harmful practices. Similarly, requiring followers to engage in several hours of meditation per day plus discouraging the questioning of "cult" doctrine have often been portrayed as parts of a group's "brainwashing" regime designed to damage one's ability to reason properly.

Once again, the problem with such criteria is that they are naive. If celibacy was harmful, for example, then how does one explain the lack of more-than-ordinary pathology among monks and nuns? Also, if certain mental practices actually damaged the brain, then why do members of intensive religious groups perform so well on I.Q. tests and other measures of individual reasoning ability? Such critical criteria also reflect an abysmal ignorance of traditional religious practices: Many traditional religions have promoted celibacy, restricted diets, prescribed lengthy prayers and meditations, discouraged the questioning of group ideology, etc. Clearly, if one wants to delineate serious criteria for determining "bad religion," then one must focus on traits that embody more than the observer's ethnocentric attitudes.

To begin with, making a radical lifestyle change as part of joining a religious group should not, in itself, be taken to indicate that the individual has therefore become involved in something harmful. Friends and family members may feel that an individual is making a mistake to quit a job or to drop out of school—actions that, by the way, very few contemporary new religions would actively encourage—but a free society means nothing if one is not also free to make mistakes.

Developing Objective Early Warning Signs

If one wishes to develop objective criteria for distinguishing harmful or potentially harmful religious organizations from harmless religions, one needs to place oneself in the position of a public policy maker. From this perspective, religions that raise the most concern are those groups that tangibly, physically harm members and/or non-members, or engage in other anti-social/illegal acts. However, a public policy maker might well respond that this post facto criterion is too little too late, and that what is needed are criteria that could act as early warning signs—criteria indicating that a previously innocuous group is potentially "going bad." The following discussion will make a stab at developing such criteria, with the caveat that the presence of the less serious factors listed below in any given group does not automatically mean they are on the verge of becoming the next Heaven's Gate.

Charismatic Leader: As part of this discussion, we shall be referring to a few false criteria for distinguishing a healthy from an unhealthy religion. In the first place, the mere fact that a group is headed up by a charismatic leader does not automatically raise a red flag. This is because new religions are much like new businesses: new businesses are almost always the manifestation of the vision and work of a single entrepreneur. In contrast, few if any successful businesses are the outgrowth of the work of a committee.

Divine Authority: Also, to found a religion, a leader usually makes some sort of claim to special insight or to special revelation that legitimates both the new religion and the leader's right to lead. The founder may even claim to be prophet, messiah or avatar. While many critics of alternative religions have asserted that the assumption of such authority is in itself a danger sign, too many objectively harmless groups have come into being with the leader asserting divine authority for such claims to be meaningful danger signs.

Use of Authority: Far more important than one's claim to authority is what one does with the authority once he or she attracts followers who choose to recognize it. A minister or guru who focuses her or his pronouncements on the interpretation of scripture or on other matters having to do with religion proper is far less problematic than a leader who takes it upon her- or himself to make decisions in the personal lives of individual parishioners, such as dictating (as opposed to suggesting) who and when one will marry. The line between advising and ordering others with respect to their personal lives can, however, be quite thin. A useful criterion for determining whether or not this line has been crossed is to examine what happens when one acts against the guru's advice: If one can respectfully disagree about a particular item of personal—as opposed to religious—advice without suffering negative consequences as a result, then the leadership dynamics within the group are healthy with respect to authority issues.

One of the clearest signs that leaders are overstepping their proper sphere of authority is when they articulate certain ethical guidelines that everyone must follow except for the guru or minister. This is especially the case with a differential sexual ethic that restricts the sexual activity of followers but allows leaders to initiate liaisons with whomever they choose.

Above the Law: Perhaps the most serious danger sign is when a religious group places itself above the law, although there are some nuances that make this point trickier than it might first appear. All of us, in some sphere of life, place ourselves above the law, if only when we go a few miles per hour over the speed limit or fudge a few figures on our income tax returns. Also, when push comes to shove, almost every religion in the world would be willing to assert that divine law takes precedence over human law—should they ever come into conflict. Hence a group that, for example, solicits donations in an area where soliciting is forbidden should not, on that basis alone, be viewed as danger to society. Exceptions should also be made for groups or individuals who make a very public protest against certain laws judged as immoral, as when a contentious objector goes to jail rather than be drafted into the military.

On the other hand, it should be clear that a group leader who consistently violates serious laws has developed a rationale that could easily be used to legitimate more serious anti-social acts. Examples that come readily to mind are Marshall Hertiff, founder/leader of Heaven's Gate, who regularly ducked out on motel bills and who was once even arrested for stealing a rental car, and Swami Kirtananda, founder of the New Vrindavan community, who was caught authorizing the stealing of computer software before being arrested for ordering the murder of a community critic. Documentable child abuse and other illegalities committed within the organization are also covered by this criterion.

End of the World Scenarios: Another misconceived criterion is perceiving groups as dangerous because of apocalyptic theologies. Almost every religion in the larger Judeo-Christian-Islamic tradition has an apocalyptic theology, even the traditional peace churches that forbid members from participating in the military. Thus, contrary to the assertions of some contemporary critics of religion, having an apocalyptic theology does not, in itself, raise a red flag. This is because in most apocalyptic scenarios it is God and his angels who fight the final battle, not flesh-and-blood human beings. The human role is spiritual, and the "saved" fight a spiritual war, not a literal, physical war.

An apocalyptic theology is only dangerous when individual followers believe they are going to be called upon to be foot soldiers in God's army, and prepare themselves by stocking up on weapons and ammunition. Groups that come to mind here are some of the Identity Christian churches who see themselves as preparing to fight a literal war with God's enemies. On the other hand, a community's possession of firearms—in the absence of such a theology of physical confrontation—is probably not dangerous, if no other danger signs are present. If the simple possession of firearms by members was a significant danger sign, then the Southern Baptist Convention would be the most dangerous "cult" in the nation.

Salvation: Another false, yet frequently voiced criterion is that religious groups are dangerous which see only themselves as saved and the rest of the world as damned. Like apocalypticism, this trait is far too widespread among traditional religions to constitute an authentic danger sign. A more meaningful characteristic should be how a religion actually treats non-members.

Group Isolation: Another criterion is a group's relative isolation. This trait is somewhat more complex than the others we have examined. On the one hand, there are abundant examples of traditional religions establishing communities or monastic centers apart from the larger society that have posed no danger to anyone. On the other hand, some of the worst abuses have taken place in the segregated (usually communal) sub-societies of certain minority religions. From the suicidal violence of People's Temple to the externally-directed violence of AUM Shinrikyo, it was the social dynamics found in an isolated or semi-isolated community that allowed such extreme actions to be contemplated.

In order to flag this characteristic while simultaneously avoiding stigmatizing every religion that sets up a segregated society as being potentially dangerous, it might be best to invert this trait and state it as a counter-indicator. In other words, rather than asserting that any religion with a partially isolated community is potentially dangerous, let us instead assert that the relative lack of such boundaries indicates that the group in question is almost certainly not dangerous.

Deception: A final early warning sign is a group's readiness to deceive outsiders. Some critics have asserted that a recruiter who invites a potential convert to a dinner without mentioning that the event is being sponsored by such-and-such church is deceptive. Others have criticized religions possessing a hierarchical system of knowledge to which only initiates are privy. These kinds of criticisms are silly. When a guru publicly asserts that no one in his organization is involved in illegal drugs and police later find a LSD laboratory in his basement, that's deception.

Warning Signs

To summarize, the traits we designated above as "early warning signs of 'bad religion'" are:

1. The organization is willing to place itself above the law. With the exceptions noted earlier, this is probably the most important characteristic.
2. The leadership dictates (rather than suggests) important personal (as opposed to spiritual) details of followers' lives, such as whom to marry, what to study in college, etc.
3. The leader sets forth ethical guidelines members must follow but from which the leader is exempt.
4. The group is preparing to fight a literal, physical Armageddon against other human beings.
5. The leader regularly makes public assertions that he or she knows is false and/or the group has a policy of routinely deceiving outsiders.

Finally, we noted that, while many benign religions establish semi-segregated communities, socially dangerous religions are almost always isolated or partially isolated from the larger society.

These five traits are about as close as one can get to legitimate, objective criteria for judging whether or not a given religious organization is going—or has gone—"bad." With the exception of placing the group's actions above the law, none of these characteristics, taken by themselves, are necessarily cause for alarm. On the other hand, a group possessing more than one or two of the above traits might well bear closer scrutiny. As a corollary to this line of analysis, minority religions possessing none of the above traits are, from a public policy standpoint, almost certainly harmless.

A SHORT HISTORY OF CULTS IN AMERICA

Donald C. Swift

American religion has become increasingly diverse in the latter part of the twentieth century. In his book *Religion and the American Experience: A Social and Cultural History,* Donald C. Swift notes the trend since the 1960s for many young people to reject conventional religious doctrine. Consequently, various new cultic groups have emerged to fill the spiritual void, he maintains, and some previously obscure noncultic religions, such as Eastern religions, have gained popularity in America. In the following excerpt from his book, Swift provides an objective sketch of prominent cults, such as the Heaven's Gate, Children of God, and Hare Krishna movements. His description of these various groups gives a broad overview of cultic activity in America in the last forty years. Swift is a professor of history at Edinboro University in Pennsylvania.

In the 1960s, some young people rejected the values of Catholics, Protestants, and Jews and turned to Eastern religion, drugs, and cults. This was an effort to replace what they viewed as the discredited values of Western civilization. Some of these movements remained very small, but George Gallup reported in the late seventies that a substantial number of people were involved to some degree in various cults and movements. Not all of them were young people. Some others were "into" various forms of meditation or followed Timothy Leary's advice on using LSD to "get out of your minds and into your senses." Therapies that promised adherents they would learn to "give themselves permission," "free themselves of shoulds," and "go with the flow" flourished among the young, but also had a significant number of older adherents. Theirs was a spiritual quest, often ending in the dead ends of substance addiction and self-indulgence.

Hundreds of thousands practiced yoga and transcendental meditation. Many did so in addition to involvement in more conventional religions. It is difficult to determine if practitioners with no involvement in conventional religion would consider meditation or yoga

Excerpted from Donald C. Swift, *Religion and the American Experience: A Social and Cultural History, 1765–1997* (Armonk, NY: M.E. Sharpe, 1998). Reprinted by permission of the publisher.

their religions. There were about 3 million Christian charismatics; these people rejected conventional modes of worship but usually adhered to conventional morality and theology. Several hundred thousand were in the Jesus Movement, but it now appears to be diminishing. Those disillusioned with the counterculture of the 1960s often found refuge there and accepted the movement's authoritarian ways and ultraconservative morality and theology. Some eventually became Jewish Christians, people who insist they are Jews but accept Christ as the Messiah.

It is estimated that there are about one thousand cults active today. The cults usually have in common a charismatic living leader, demands for fanatical loyalty and obedience, recruitment practices of debatable propriety, and insistence that members surrender all assets and raise money for them. In several instances the ultimate test of loyalty and obedience was acceptance of death and suicide. In 1978, nine hundred members of the People's Temple accepted mass suicide in Jonestown, Guyana. Most of them were poor African Americans from San Francisco, initially attracted by leader Jim Jones's mixture of concern for economic and social justice with Pentecostal religion. Prior to the massacre or mass suicide, Jones encountered difficulties with Guyanan and American authorities over violence and threats against opponents and dissenters, reports of sexual abuse of women and children, and evidence that he ordered the murder of a visiting congressman, Leo Ryan. Jones instructed his followers to drink Kool-Aid laced with cyanide; he opted to die of a 38 caliber bullet fired into the head.

Jones originally thought it best to die in a blazing inferno, but it remained for over seventy Branch Davidian followers of David Koresh to die that way in April 1993 at their compound near Waco, Texas. Koresh taught an adventist theology, and was sexually involved with many of the women and girls he led; he aroused the interest of federal authorities by stockpiling arms and weapons.

At Rancho Santa Fe, California, in March 1997, thirty-nine members of the Heaven's Gate cult committed suicide so that God would transport them several days later to a UFO they thought followed in the wake of the Hale-Bopp comet. They believed the spaceship would take them to heavenly bliss on another planet. They were led by Marshall H. Applewhite and Bonnie Lu Trusdale Nettles, who called themselves Bo and Peep, Winnie and Pooh, Chip and Dale, or the Two. Though they claimed to be acquainted in previous lives, they met in their most recent incarnation in a hospital in the early 1970s, where Nettles was a nurse and he, as a heart-blockage patient, had a "near death" experience. Nettles helped him define his mission, traveled with him in seeking followers, and she finally died of cancer. Applewhite referred to himself as "the Present Representation" of the spirit that animated Christ in the New Testament and warned that planet Earth was about to be recycled. He preached celibacy, and he and some of the males in the cult had been castrated; the members dressed to effect a unisex look. These people earned money as computer technicians and used a Web site to spread their views and recruit members. Apparently, each member was given an opportunity to leave rather than commit suicide. Other members of the cult survived elsewhere.

Two of the more notable cults did not begin as religions. Synanon, founded by Chuck Dederich, emerged in California in the 1960s as a community that taught love, peace, healing, and nonviolence. Initially accomplishing positive change in the lives of street people and derelicts, it eventually moved to requiring vasectomies of male members, redefining marriage, gathering weapons, and using force against dissenters and opponents. Dederich intimidated the media by filing suits against the *San Francisco Examiner* and other critics. It may have become a religion to gain First Amendment protection against governmental interference. In 1980, it had few members and was in decline.

Scientology was founded in 1951 by L. Ronald Hubbard as a science somewhat akin to psychology. It is based on the idea that liberating the soul requires locating and healing "engrams," emotional scars from a previous life or one's present life, including the fetal stage. It evolved into a religion and taught that the spirit or "thetan" is immortal and inhabits a succession of human bodies. Scientologists do not remove themselves from society but seek ways to function more efficiently in it. They take courses costing as much as $300 an hour from the Church of Scientology. This movement is probably the most powerful of the cults, even though it has faced litigation for kidnapping, swindling, and breaking into federal offices. Mary Sue Hubbard, the founder's wife, spent several years in prison for obstruction of justice. The Internal Revenue Service spent twenty years scrutinizing the operations of the church, but both sides appear to have arrived at a settlement in 1997.

Both Synanon and Scientology are non-Christian and reflect what is called New Age thought, and have been particularly strong on the West Coast. The Heaven's Gate group is another example of New Age religion. Adherents of New-Age thought seek esoteric knowledge to provide them with a comprehensive explanation of the universe and their place in it. New Age religion is a form of theosophy, which draws on Eastern wisdom, gnosticism, and astrology. Crystals are sometimes used to deepen knowledge, and ancient Celtic wisdom is sought through study of the Druids. New Age includes various forms of goddess worship, which has a growing following in feminist circles and has been welcomed by the Unitarian Universalist Association. New Age thought seeks to liberate the inner self, considered perfect but contaminated by the "lower self" or "outer personality," which is shaped by materialism and modernity.

Some New Age movements attempt to provide followers with the best of both material and spiritual worlds. Werner Erhard's seminars emphasize the importance of positive external achievements while seeking inner enlightenment. A slogan associated with guru Bhagwan Shree Rajneesh proclaims, "Jesus saves, Moses invests, Bhagwan spends." It is thought that fewer than fifty thousand people seriously consider New Age thought to be their religion, though a much greater number have dabbled in it. Some place the number of people who have been exposed to New Age thought between 10 and 12 million. There are about one hundred New Age periodicals, and about $100 million worth of New Age books are sold each year. There are even some New Age radio stations. Some of the young, especially those involved in radical politics, view Christianity and Judaism as the tribal religions of a bankrupt Western civilization; to endorse them is to endorse racism, militarism, imperialism, and capitalism, and anything else is preferable.

Children of God and Other Movements

At its peak, there were about ten thousand Children of God, who came to believe that former Baptist minister David Berg was the Messiah. By 1974, they claimed to have 120 communes in the United States. Berg took the name Moses Berg, claimed revelations from God, and began writing letters to replace the Bible. Twice, he unsuccessfully predicted the end of the world, but followers continued to collect money and study the gospel of "Mo." Accused in the 1970s of advocating prostitution on the part of female members, incest, opposition to marriage, and irregular financial dealings, Berg began moving his followers to Europe, but his disciples still recruit in the United States, often using aliases such as the Christian Faith Movement.

The Unification Church was founded in 1951 in South Korea by Sun Myung Moon, who claimed to be a messiah. He said that he learned this in a vision in which Christ, the Messiah of the first Advent, spoke to him. Using some elements of Taoism and Buddhism, Moon preached repentance, claiming that he could redeem the world if the church were successful in unifying and governing it. Claiming to be "Lord of the Second Advent," Moon could succeed where Jesus Christ had failed. To accomplish his mission he moved to the United States, where he had forty thousand followers by the early 1980s and church-owned businesses worth about $100 million. Moon spent some time in prison on tax evasion charges. His church does not avoid political involvement, and it owns one of the two major newspapers in Washington, D.C.

Swami Prabhupada was sixty-one years old in 1966 when he came to America and founded the International Society of Krishna Consciousness, also known as Hare Krishna. This meditative religion focuses on the worship of three deities, Brahma, Vishnu, and Shiva. Lord Krishna was the eighth incarnation of Vishnu, and is honored by dancing, chanting, and singing. Worship in these forms, it is claimed, drives ignorance from the human soul. The word "Hare" in Hindu religions means "the energy of God." Followers avoid eating meat, shun luxuries, and practice strict asceticism, usually in monastic communities. Men and women are often segregated, and sex and marriage are not encouraged. The movement supports itself through the sale of flowers, incense, buttons, and literature. Though there could be several thousand members at a given time, tens of thousands of middle-class young people have passed through it. Hindus of all persuasions accounted for three-tenths of a percent of the population in 1990.

Prior drug use often was associated with the decision to join Hare Krishna and other new religions. Through drugs, some felt they had religious experiences, which they sought to revive or continue without drugs in morally conservative movements such as Hare Krishna, the Unification Church, or the Jesus People.

Judeo-Christian dominance was challenged by numerous Muslims and adherents of Eastern religions. About 2 million belonged to Eastern religions, but most of them were immigrants from Asia. It is notable, however, that half the Koreans living in the United States are Presbyterians. Most were Presbyterian before coming here, and some converted after they arrived. Korean Americans have over 1,200 Presbyterian churches, as well as 500 Southern Baptist and 250 United Methodist churches. These Korean Christians work hard, are economically successful, and see their churches as centers of community life. Their Christianity facilitates assimilation. About half of Asian immigrants are Christian; most are Protestant, but Filipinos are predominantly Roman Catholic.

There are many varieties of Buddhism in the United States. Among them are Zen Buddhists from many countries, and the separatist and authoritarian Nichiren Shoshu Soka Gakkai from Japan, who claim the ability to cure and transform lives, including economically. Entertainer Tina Turner is probably the best-known of its American converts. Many Americans have embraced Zen Buddhism, and today only a fifth of American Zen centers are led by Asians. Allan Watts, a practitioner and advocate of Zen, holds that it has two aspects, "square Zen," or discipline and meditation, and "beat Zen," the sense of total liberation.

Forty-seven organizations were represented at the 1988 American Buddhist Congress in Los Angeles. American Buddhism tends to center on the laity and avoids the traditional emphasis on a hierarchy of monks. It also attempts to meet the concerns of women. There were some sexual and financial scandals in the 1980s. Buddhism appears to be losing many to Christianity, agnosticism, and secular humanism.

There are over four hundred thousand Hindus, who usually worship in their homes rather than in temples. In the 1960s and 1970s, a substantial number of Americans traveled to India in search of inner peace and enlightenment by studying with gurus, such as Bhagwan Shree Rajneesh.

By 1995, it was estimated that there were between 4.6 million and 5 million Muslims in the United States and Canada. There are in excess of a thousand Islamic centers and about half a million mosqued Muslims. The largest numbers of Muslims worship in New York, southern California, Chicago, Washington, and Toronto. Multicultural congregations are to be found in 70 percent of the mosques. The largest groups of Muslims are African Americans or Indo-Pakistanis; Arab Americans are the third largest group. One-fifth of the mosques follow Imam W. Deen Mohammed, who brought the Black Muslims into the orthodox Muslim movement. The Islamic Society of North America claims the adherence of 40 percent of the mosques, and the remaining mosques are unaffiliated.

Most American Muslims belong to the Sunni sect of Islam, but there are numerous followers of the more fundamentalist and often militant Shiite sect. The process of assimilation frequently blurs the distinctions between these sects. The oldest standing mosque in the United States is in Cedar Rapids. Beginning as a community center for Muslims, it became a mosque in 1934 and is known as the Mother Mosque of America. Today members of the Cedar Rapids Islamic community are proud of how well they have assimilated; some have married outside their faith. Muslims, particularly of the first generation, oppose pornography, sex outside the family, and abortion. They adhere to family values that are quite similar to those of conservative Christians and Jews. Like other first-generation parents, they are concerned that their children remain faithful to their religion and its values.

Feminist witchcraft is another recent development. Its adherents reject traditional Judaism and Christianity and claim that women have a higher nature than men. They worship the deity of the earth, the Goddess, whom they sometimes call Sophia. They believe that women participate in her divine nature. One of their most prominent practitioners is Starhawk, who teaches that the Goddess is the source of life and "is nature [and] is flesh." To better get in touch with their natures, some worshipers of the Goddess use Tarot cards and astrology.

Mainline Protestant churches have suffered significant declines in membership and attendance, and a much smaller percentage of Roman Catholics attend mass every Sunday than at the end of World War II. Nevertheless, it is clear that there is no decline in religiosity in the United States as it approaches the twenty-first century. Religiosity is being expressed in the growth of Pentecostal and evangelical bodies and in increased interest in unconventional approaches to spirituality. The great interest in sects, the occult, and unconventional approaches to Christianity suggests that many people find that mainstream religious bodies are not meeting their needs.

CULTS: THE GREAT AMERICAN TRADITION

Sean Wilentz

According to Sean Wilentz, today's cults are products of America's rich history of religious eccentricity. Indeed, he writes, America was founded by religious dissenters seeking refuge from persecution in their native lands; committed to religious liberty, the country has long been a hotbed for cult-like groups. Wilentz disagrees with those who blame the emergence of cults on the 1960s counterculture, the Internet, or other recent developments. Rather, he argues, modern cults should be viewed as the latest in a long line of American cultic movements that, then as now, continue to appeal to a religiously diverse population. Wilentz teaches history at Princeton University. He is the co-author of *The Kingdom of Matthias: A Story of Sex and Salvation in Nineteenth-Century America.*

The cult's charismatic leader called himself Matthias the Prophet and claimed he was the latest incarnation of the Holy Spirit—a descendant of the ancient Hebrew prophets and patriarchs, including Jesus Christ. He lived communally with about 20 of his disciples—men, women and children—in a fine suburban house adjoining a spacious, well-manicured estate. Every day, the disciples listened intently to Matthias' furious, meandering sermons about the rapidly approaching Doomsday; and they obeyed his every command, including his rearrangements of the group's sexual pairings. Not surprisingly, the bearded prophet took the prettiest of the women, the wife of a wealthy disciple, as his personal "match spirit."

Outsiders suspected that awful things were happening at Mount Zion, the name Matthias gave to the commune. But only after a sickly member of the cult died under mysterious circumstances did local authorities apprehend the prophet and confirm some of the worst of the rumors.

The affair quickly became a media circus. Tabloid newspapers reported sensational details about the cult's sexual depravity and religious brainwashing. Editorial writers bemoaned Matthias' alluring

Reprinted from Sean Wilentz, "A Nation of Cults: The Great American Tradition," *Los Angeles Times*, April 6, 1997, with permission from the author.

fanaticism, and commented darkly about the state of the American psyche. And the public eagerly awaited the prophet's public trial in connection with his follower's strange demise.

It all could have happened yesterday, in Waco or in Rancho Santa Fe. Yet, the kingdom of Matthias did not rise and fall in some New Age Sunbelt outpost, but in the town of Sing Sing, N.Y., just north of New York City—in the middle of the 1830s. And though he got more attention than most, Matthias was only one of the dozens of American cult leaders who emerged over the decades following the American Revolution.

Evaluations of more recent cults, including the suicidal Heaven's Gate group, usually slight America's rich history of religious eccentricity. Some pundits are quick to blame the 1960s counterculture for spawning interest in outlandish religious doctrines. Others blame television and the Internet. Still others hypothesize that the approach of the year 2000 has led to an epidemic of millennial credulity.

Yet, if these present-minded commentaries contain some truth, they also obscure the deeper American origins of religious cultism. Founded by religious dissenters, the United States has long been a hotbed of sectarian enthusiasm. And the current explosion of millenarianism has yet to match the one that occurred amid the so-called Second Great Awakening after the Revolution—one of the most intense outbursts of religious and pseudo-religious invention since the Protestant Reformation.

Most of the early American shamans and seers made a quick impression, only to disappear into obscurity—or, as in Matthias' case, into ignominy. In the 1790s, for example, a former British army officer (his name is lost to posterity) claimed the gift of prophecy and assembled a divinely inspired political movement in Vermont and Massachusetts—but, just as rapidly, the prophet dispersed his group and was never heard from again. After the War of 1812, a band of religious seekers who called themselves Pilgrims migrated from Woodstock, Vt., (where they won at least 100 converts) to the outskirts of Troy, N.Y., and then moved again, by stages, until they reached the promised land of Missouri and faded into the countryside.

At about the same time, also in Vermont, members of a short-lived sect called the New Israelites, led by a man named Justis Winchell, declared that they had the God-given power to discover "vast quantities" of gold and silver, sufficient "to pave the streets of the New Jerusalem." A bit later, a self-declared divine monarch named James Jesse Strange ruled over a band of followers, mostly women, on Beaver Island in Lake Michigan, until he fell victim to an assassin's bullet.

Some of the early American sects—most notably the Shakers— enjoyed spectacular growth through the middle of the 19th century before fading into near-extinction. A handful of other sects, however, evolved into major religions. The most famous of these, the Church of Jesus Christ of Latter-day Saints (better known as the Mormons) got its start in upstate New York in 1819, when Jesus and God appeared in a column of white fire to the farm boy Joseph Smith. Twelve years after Smith's first vision, William Miller, a Baptist minister in Low Hampton, N.Y., announced that Christ would return to Earth in 1843, and attracted untold thousands of believers. The Millerites suffered a great disappointment when their leader's calculations proved faulty, but a number of them regrouped in the 1860s to help found the Seventh-day Adventist Church.

Then as now, the cults were hardly monolithic, doctrinally or emotionally, but they shared some common traits. They attracted a diverse following. Matthias' little group, for example, included a poor ex-slave woman and an Irish serving girl, as well as some of the most favored young members of Manhattan's mercantile elite. Cults often enforced discipline among the devout by prescribing some sort of unorthodox sexual regimen, ranging from celibacy to polygamy. Their teachings tended to focus on the attainment of some higher state of human existence, prefatory to God's destruction of the sinful world. And, as recent historians have shown, they translated into a biblical vernacular the widespread hopes, hurts and apprehensions of a rapidly changing America—a new nation experiencing intense commercial development, the demise of traditional aristocratic patriarchy and the rise of what would become familiar as sentimental Victorian sexual norms.

The most startling difference between today's cults and their early American forerunners is the modern proclivity for mass suicide. In the 19th century, believers hoped to hasten the coming of God's kingdom by perfecting human life on Earth; at the end of the 20th, there is a tendency to want to leave Earth altogether—to be transported (perhaps by UFOs, the modern equivalent of celestial angels) directly to kingdom come.

But in other respects, the modern cults are best approached not as some bizarre, turn-of-the-millennium outburst but as the latest in a long line of American millenarian movements. Where they will lead is by no means certain. But it should surprise nobody if one of today's prophets—perhaps the late L. Ron Hubbard—turns out to have been a latter-day Joseph Smith, the founder of a full-fledged respectable religion. And if the outcome of the Matthias cult's story, among many others, is indicative, we should learn to expect the unexpected from America's ever volatile sectarian life.

As it happened, Matthias was acquitted of murdering his follower, though he wound up serving time on some lesser charges. He was last seen preaching to Indians in Iowa Territory in the early 1840s.

Yet, that was not quite the end of the affair. After the prophet's release from jail, his most loyal disciple, the ex-slave Isabella, heard new commandments from God. Some years later, she became a famous advocate of abolitionism and feminism, under a new heavenly name: Sojourner Truth. But that, as they say, is another story.

CHAPTER 2

THE PROCESS OF CONVERSION

CULT RECRUITMENT

Margaret Thaler Singer

Margaret Thaler Singer is a clinical psychologist who has counseled many former cult members and has conducted extensive
research on cultic groups. Based on her observations, Singer
believes that anyone can be vulnerable to the recruitment process
typically used by cults. In the following selection, taken from her
book *Cults in Our Midst,* Singer explains how cults use intense and
often sophisticated psychological control methods to recruit and
convert new members. First, according to Singer, cult recruiters
employ verbal seduction and charm to lure new members to the
group. When recruits express interest, the cult uses manipulation,
isolation, and trickery to solidify its hold on new members, she
reports. These deceptive practices, Singer argues, belie the claim
that members join cults of their own free will.

All of us are vulnerable to cult recruitment. So many cults, using so
many guises and ploys, are actively looking for members at any given
moment that surely there may be a cult for you. Whatever your age,
whatever your interests, whatever your life-style, succumbing to the
lure of a cult recruiter is as easy as getting a library card. There are as
many ways to become involved with a cult as there are cults.

Each group develops its own recruitment methods—ranging from
personal contacts to advertisements on kiosks, in newspapers and
magazines, and on television and radio. The original point of recruitment may vary, but one constant factor is that rampant deceptions
are involved. These deceptions extend from concealment of exactly
what the group is at "the point of pick up" to concealment of the ultimate purpose of membership.

Someone may try to get you into a cult by contacting you on your
computer bulletin board. You may sign up for a college class only to
find that the instructor is a dedicated cultist, bent on surreptitiously
recruiting students. You may visit your veterinarian, your chiroprac-
tor, your dentist, your optometrist, or your next-door neighbor, only
to have her or him attempt to recruit you. In a recent survey of 381
former members of 101 different cultic groups, 66 percent stated that

their initial contact with their group came through a friend or relative. The rest were recruited by strangers.

Cult recruitment occurs in four main stages: the first approach by a cult recruiter; the invitation to a wonderful place or special event or an important, alluring meeting; the first contact with the cult, where you are made to feel loved and wanted; and the follow-up, using psychologically persuasive techniques to ensure your quick return or greater commitment.

First Approach

Cult members are trained in persuasive methods of approaching potential recruits. Because we are all social creatures, most of us are prone to listen to nice-looking people who approach us in a friendly or helping manner and speak enthusiastically about what they believe in.

I have had a few persons tell me that when they were "down and out" on the streets of Los Angeles or San Francisco, they were recruited by sincere-sounding, street-preaching types, using heavy guilt and fear tactics related to the homeless person's drug and alcohol use. But what actually got them to check the group out was the personal offer of a place to stay, food, and companions who were not also on the streets. Both the sugar-and-honey and the "you must leave this sordid life" approaches are appealing because the solicitor offers something that the person feels would be good for her or him.

By and large, cult members did not seek out the group they joined but were personally approached in some way. A few persons get into cults by responding to advertisements, but even then, what ties the knot is the personal interaction with recruiters—individuals zealously focused on getting more members into the group.

Whom Do Cults Recruit?

The key vulnerability factors are, first, being in between important affiliations, between commitments to work, school, or life in general, and second, being even slightly depressed or a bit lonely. Cults aim their recruitment at vulnerable people because these individuals are less likely to see through the layers of deceit. Cults target friendly, obedient, altruistic, and malleable persons because such individuals are easy to persuade and manage. Cults prefer not to deal with recalcitrant, disobedient, self-centered types, for they are simply too difficult to mold and control.

Another important factor is that the person approached by a cult recruiter must see that there is time available to check out the recruiter's proposal. Also, he or she must resonate to the offering. This means the recruiter must manipulate the first conversation, getting enough information about the person to shape the discussion and make the group seem like something the person would want to know about or experience.

Where Do Cults Recruit?

Cults recruit everywhere. They hold lectures, seminars, retreats, revivals, and meetings of all sorts, and they go door to door. They run schools, universities, health clinics, and businesses. They advertise in New Age magazines, in alternative newspapers, and in business journals. They have tables at professional and trade meetings, computer expositions, publishing exhibitions, and street fairs. One large cult has a rock band that tours the country and serves as an attraction in malls and large assembly areas. Of course, cult members also recruit among their own family circles, friendship networks, co-workers, and vocational or hobby associations.

Although cults are active everywhere, schools and university campuses have been a fertile field for recruitment for all types of cults since the sixties. Some cults assign members to recruit on junior and senior high school grounds, in college dormitories and at freshmen activities days, and at all sorts of campus events and locales.

In the survey mentioned earlier, of the 381 former members, 43 percent were students when they were recruited (10 percent in high school, 27 percent in college, and 6 percent in graduate school), and 38 percent of these students dropped out of school once they'd joined the group.

Here, for example, is the experience of one college student.

> "Charles," a university senior active in a number of social and political causes, felt he could handle any verbal challenges that came his way. He was bright, educated, articulate, and before this experience, would never have dreamed he could get caught up in a cult.
>
> "Barnabas," the leader of a small cult, had written to a university official saying that he operated an international foundation and was looking for an outstanding student to include on his team. Without any exploration into the validity of this claim, an administrator sent the letter to a department head who gave Charles's name to the cult leader. Barnabas sought out Charles and introduced himself, stating that he headed a peace foundation and wanted to put students in charge of segments of the new world order.
>
> Tall, demanding, articulate, and energetic, Barnabas managed to impress Charles and several other students who agreed to work with him. Barnabas soon wore them down through long, haranguing, sleep-depriving sessions conducted in their residence hall. He showed up at Charles's classes, sat beside him, and did not let him out of his sight. Soon, Charles left school to trek up and down the West Coast with Barnabas,

stopping at automatic teller machines for Charles to withdraw cash for bus tickets and meals. Barnabas also got other
students to leave school.

Cults use a variety of strategies and change them as needed in
order to increase their possibilities for success. Former members have
told me how, from time to time, their leaders changed tactics,
announcing that certain ploys would work better.

For example, an interesting change of methods was described by
a woman who had been trained by her Bible cult leader to go to college dorms and eating areas, approach women students who were
alone, and start conversations with them to get them to attend
"study groups." One day, her cult leader abruptly changed procedures. Up to that point, individual members had gone out seeking
people of the same sex. "Now," the leader proclaimed, "we will have
team gathering and reaping. From now on, two sisters or two brothers will go out as pairs to gather and reap, and that way they can
approach both men and women." The leader said it was "too sexual" for a man to be approached by a lone woman, or a woman to be
approached by a lone man, but two women or two men made such
an approach "friendship," and the teams would be able to recruit
both male and female students faster. The woman said the new
method worked.

Each cult develops its own methods. Some have manuals on how
to recruit and provide special training for those members assigned to
recruitment. One group sends recruiters out to "look for raw meat";
some have recruitment quotas for each member. Other cults tell
members to write up lists of everyone they know and then approach
those people to join. Cult leadership helps members refine their
recruitment approaches and identify weak spots in the prospective
members, based on descriptions in written reports. There is no limit
to the ingenuity and also the trickery used. Former cult members
often tell me that they didn't even notice their first fatal step toward
joining because so much deception was involved.

I have also had people say to me, "No one could argue me into one
of those weird groups!" to which I usually respond, "That's right.
Arguing is not very seductive. Charm and flattery are." Then I ask,
"Did someone ever induce you to go to something, to do something,
to believe something that you later found out was a 'line'?" Most
people have had such an experience and when they think of the
recruitment process that way can understand it a little better.

Invitation

Once contact with a prospective member is made, the pursuit may go
something like this:

First, the recruiter, appearing nonthreatening, learns something
about the potential recruit in order to put into play the idea that the

recruiter and the recruit are alike, that they share commonalities and are in sync.

Second, through this process, the recruiter gets the potential recruit to feel that he or she is resonating with this nice person who is showing such personal care and interest.

Third, the recruiter mirrors the interests and attitudes of the potential recruit, whether these interests are spirituality, nursing, political change, music, or any other area. The recruiter then demonstrates that he has something to offer the potential recruit by extending a verbal invitation to an event, a class, or a dinner.

A *front group* is an organization that serves as a false front for another operation that remains behind the scenes. Most cults have front groups, sometimes a variety of them, set up specifically to appeal to a range of interests. Among these front groups are instructional classes, study groups, Bible groups, social clubs, hobby organizations, management- or job-related training seminars, grass-roots activities, neighborhood associations, political committees, sales schemes, meditation or yoga classes, travel clubs, workers' groups, weight-loss programs, medical offices, psychotherapy clinics, and printing and publishing collectives.

Generally, when a person goes to the first event, he or she sees no indication of a connection to a cult or some background organization. Often even the leader's name doesn't come up until some time after the recruit is drawn further into the recruitment web.

Street Recruitment

On several occasions I have gone out on the streets of Berkeley near the University of California campus with a former cult member who had been a very successful street recruiter. I would be present as she did her old pitch, just as she did in the cult, to get a stranger on the street to promise to come that night or sometime soon to a lecture, a dinner, a meeting for a political cause, or an event focused on ecology issues, self-improvement, or the UFO phenomenon. We targeted non-student types, making test cases of the over-thirty crowd—businesspeople and professors, both men and women—to assess how a sophisticated and well-educated audience would respond. Marveling, I would watch my friend work the technique she had learned in the cult. She would talk with a person on the street for a short time; then after the person agreed to come to an event, my friend would introduce me, saying that I was a professor studying cults and that, since she had been in a certain cult and spent much time recruiting, she was showing me exactly how it worked. The people who had been approached were astonished. "But I believed you!" they would exclaim. "You seem like such a nice person. You couldn't have been in a cult."

Often the person who had been approached would ask, "But how did you know I would be interested in a peace group?" or whichever lure had worked. My friend would then repeat her questions and the person's answers, showing how she had capitalized on clues to get a bit more information, and then had made her offer match what the person had unwittingly indicated an interest in. She would explain that she had done the pitch exactly as she had when she recruited for the cult and that it was the standard pitch taught in that group. We would then thank the person and say we hoped he or she had profited from seeing how easily anyone can be tricked and persuaded with soft talk, charm, and an interesting, appealing topic, all of which could be a fabrication—or step one to joining a cult. Almost without fail, each person remarked, "Is that how it's done? It was so smooth. Seemed so honest. I thought cults harangued people with sin, or enlightenment, or something, and argued with them to join."

That First Fatal Step

Many former cult members have referred to "that first fatal step." As they look back, they realize that, for a combination of reasons, their first step of acquiescing to an invitation or a request was the start of weeks, months, or years in a cult. In most cases, potential recruits are pressed to attend an event right away. The recruiter says the event is perfect for them, and gives them no time to reflect on whether they really want to go. Here's a specific example of the way this first step can work.

> "Mike" was in his thirties when he came to Berkeley to study for the California Bar Exam. One day, he was approached by two charming women who said they lived in an "international communal living group" that had a place near the snow country. The women were "so personal, so personable, so charming, so clean-looking, so sincere," and their pitch was so seductive, so urgent, and so singularly appealing, that within three hours he had taken them to his apartment, gotten his camera, his ski equipment, some of his study materials, and his certificate of ownership for his car. He said later that, at the time, he did not even question why they wanted him to bring the deed to his car.

> They had convinced him that he could study at their retreat. They promised him that he would have his own cabin and good food and that other law students would be there. They said there would be some lectures about their group but assured him he could spend time studying.

> Mike spent nearly ten days in the country. His stay ended only when he threatened that if his car was not produced and he was not allowed to leave he would file legal charges

against the group. All the visible telephones were broken, and "visitors" were not permitted into the leaders' building to use the working phones. He never had one moment alone the entire time. When, after three days, he realized the group was really a religious cult, he said he wanted to leave. But suddenly, they couldn't locate his car or his ski equipment and camera. When he finally got his car, which they claimed had been moved some miles across the property to a safe place, he drove off leaving behind his other valuables. He was simply relieved to get away.

Former cult members have told me that what they were told, what they read, and what they experienced on first meeting the recruiter had enough appeal at that point in their lives that it hooked them—in more ways than one. The hook was a combination of their own needs at the time and the personality and approach of the recruiter, plus the fact that the topic the recruiter mentioned clicked with them. The recruiter also convinced them they had the time to check it out, and they were convinced that they needed what was being offered.

First Cult Contact

Cults are not like most groups we know in our society. On the surface they may seem like mundane groups, but they differ in many ways. Joining a cult is not like joining the local country club, the Baptist Church, or a Rotary Club, or like taking employment with a commercial enterprise or legitimate nonprofit organization. These latter groups want you to know just who they are and what their program is; they want full capacity, informed consent from you before you join or take the job.

Cults are also reminiscent of a jack-in-the-box—a pretty, innocuous-looking container that, when opened, surprises you with a pop-out figure, often a scary one. Similarly, surprising and frightening things pop out over the course of membership in a cult. What you first see is not what's inside.

Some groups invite you to a meal, claiming to be campus peace organizations when in fact they are fronts for an international cult. They invite you to the country for a three-day seminar. Then, once you're there, they ask you to stay for a one-week program, then another one for twenty-one days. After that amount of time, you'll be so inculcated with their ideas that they'll be able to send you out on the streets to collect money and enlist new members. Within a month or so of their first involvement, . . . most recruits are caught.

Recruits are brought to camps in the country, weekend retreats, clandestine cult facilities, workshops in the desert, and a host of other places to isolate them from access to their usual social life. Cult leaders and heads of other groups using thought-reform processes know that this change of place is a practical and effective means of quickly changing behavior and conduct. When cut off from social support, social background, families, familiar surroundings, friends, jobs, schoolmates, and classes and brought into new environs with a new ambience, few can resist the pull to fit in.

Love Bombing

Most cults have specific plans for drawing in each recruit. As soon as any interest is shown by the recruits, they may be *love bombed* by the recruiter or other cult members. This process of feigning friendship and interest in the recruit was initially associated with one of the early youth cults, but soon it was taken up by a number of groups as part of their program for luring people in. Love bombing is a coordinated effort, usually under the direction of leadership, that involves long-term members' flooding recruits and newer members with flattery, verbal seduction, affectionate but usually nonsexual touching, and lots of attention to their every remark. Love bombing—or the offer of instant companionship—is a deceptive ploy accounting for many successful recruitment drives.

In addition, the newcomer is surrounded by long-term members. Not only are these more experienced members trained to love bomb the potential recruit, but they are on their best behavior, proudly proclaiming the joys of membership, the advantages of the new belief system, and the uniqueness of the leader. Consciously or unconsciously, these members always speak and make their presentations in cult jargon, which they all seem to understand but which tends to make the newcomer feel out of sorts, a bit alienated, and undereducated by cult standards. The lonely visitor or seminar attendee begins to want some sense of connection to the rest of the group. With all the surrounding reinforcement, soon enough the newcomer realizes that, in order to be accepted and part of the group, she or he simply needs to mirror the behavior of other members and imitate their language.

Because many groups use this tactic of having older members train and watch over recruits and newer members, recruits are never alone and cannot talk freely with other recruits. Immediately, the cult's training program and the thought-reform atmosphere, reinforced by the modeling behavior of older members, prevents recruits and new members from challenging the system. There is no opportunity for doubts or negative feelings to be supported, corroborated, or validated. In one way or another, in every kind of cult, recruits are told that negativity is never to be expressed. Should they have any questions, hesitations, or bad feelings, they are told to consult with an upper-level person, or their trainer, helper, or guide. Isolated from others who have doubts and questions, recruits are left with the impression that everyone else agrees with what is going on.

The complete attention of the newcomers is engaged through a heavy schedule of such activities as playing games, attending lectures, group singing, doing collective work, studying basic texts, joining picket lines, going on fund-raising drives, or completing various assigned tasks, such as writing a personal autobiography for examination by the group. In this way, recruits are kept occupied to such a degree that they don't get around to thinking about what they are doing or what is being done to them.

Follow-Up: Gaining Greater Commitment

When some people think of cult recruitment, they picture a ranting, wild-eyed zealot. This image is a far cry from the sophistication of the actual recruitment process. Effective cult leaders and recruiters verbally seduce, charm, manipulate, and trick people into taking that first fatal step and then into making increasing commitments to the group. The selling of the cult's program proceeds by means of calculated persuasion procedures. And these recruitment and conversion practices belie the cults' claim that people freely join them. Most recruits have little real knowledge of what will eventually happen to them, and it's rare for a new member to exercise anything like fully informed consent in making the decision to join. More likely, he or she makes an emotionally based acquiescence to complex, powerful, and organized persuasion tactics.

As new members are gradually exposed to the series of classes, events, and/or experiences that will, one step at a time, cut them off from their pasts and the world as they knew it and change them so gradually that they won't notice, they are also often kept awake for long periods doing their work assignments, studying, listening to lectures, meditating, chanting, and so on. Soon they become sleep-deficient, which further disturbs their critical faculties. Lack of food or sudden changes in diet cause yet other incapacities and confusion. Before long, recruits immersed in this new environment are, without realizing it, beginning to think in a new way.

In addition, cults control the information flow for all members. They may control ingoing and outgoing correspondence, telephone calls, radio or television use, unauthorized reading matter, visits by outsiders, and trips to the outside. In some cults, the telephones just happen to be broken; in others, especially in the political cults, use of phones is restricted as a "security" precaution. In the end, members' contacts with former ties are either completely cut off or strongly discouraged by both leadership and peers. To avoid disfavor and conflict, recruits go along with the program.

Manipulation and Deception

Manipulation of thoughts and feelings is central to the success of the cult recruitment process. Cults play upon normal feelings of ambivalence, and this is especially successful with young people, who have less life experience. For example, it is almost impossible for adolescents and young adults not to have mixed feelings about their parents. Even the most beloved mothers and fathers have had encounters with their children that leave memories of anger or disappointment, and most parents have at least a few irritating habits or peculiarities. Many cults make a point of tapping into these unresolved feelings and exploiting them to bind members to the group.

Some cults also use dress or other external features as visible symbols in converting newcomers to the cult's ways. If you really want to change people, change their appearance. Thus cult members can be asked or told to cut their hair or wear it in a particular style, wear different clothes, take on new names, and assume certain gestures or mannerisms. One large cult, for example, has its members adopt vegetarianism, wear light-colored clothing, and chant. New members are taught to regard their mothers and fathers as "flesh-eating parents who wear ungodly clothing, intellectualize, and are unenlightened." Cult members soon cut off ties with flesh-eaters; wear light-colored clothes; avoid reflective, critical thinking about anything, much less the group; and occupy their time with almost continuous internal chanting.

Some groups also take advantage of certain coincidences, exploiting them as divine happenings to bolster faith in the group ideology and convince recruits that a meeting or simple happenstance was a predestined event. For example, some cult members on very poorly balanced diets appear pink-checked and youthful, until one notices their faces seem chapped and covered with tiny pinhead lesions, which some dermatologists tell me suggest a vitamin A deficiency. The cult, however, interprets this skin discomfort as an indication that the members have become "children of Father," "children of God," and are now "Baby Christians." In another example, a woman's brother, who lived out of town, came to the cult house to visit her while she was working her shift in a cult-owned factory. For this reason she missed seeing him, but cult officials told her, "See, the Divine Plan willed it that you must not see your brother."

On occasion, recruits are even put into brief trance states. Most people don't realize that a person can be hypnotized in simple and subtle ways, without the spectacular commands used by hypnotists who perform onstage. Someone can get you to totally concentrate on something such as an imaginary scene while he or she softly repeats subtle suggestions. Soon you will pretty much eliminate critical thinking and fall into a mild temporary trance. Through a specific, deliberate program, cult recruits and members at times can be put or fall into changed states of consciousness, which contribute to their gradually becoming restricted in their thinking.

Reflective, critical, evaluative thought, especially that critical of the cult, becomes aversive and avoided. The member will appear as you or

I do, and will function well in ordinary tasks, but the cult lectures and procedures tend to gradually induce members to experience anxiety whenever they critically evaluate the cult. Soon they are conditioned to avoid critical thinking, especially about the cult, because doing so becomes associated with pangs of anxiety and guilt.

Inducing Guilt

As part of the process of inducing guilt, all the recruit's former personal connections are deemed satanic or evil by the cult and are shown to be "against the chosen way." Since nonbelievers are bad, all relations with parents, friends, and other nonmembers are supposed to be halted. Any weakness in this area is considered very bad. The ultimate effect is that recruits assume a deep feeling of guilt about their pasts. Besides having their families and personal relationships condemned, recruits are also led to believe that they themselves were "bad people" before joining the group. Guilt feelings are produced en masse in cults.

Even more guilt is induced as recruits are set up to believe that if they ever leave the group all their ancestors and descendants will be damned or they themselves will die a pitiful death or become losers or lost souls. In this way, anxiety is heaped upon the guilt. Just as the initial love bombing awakened feelings of warmth, acceptance, and worthiness, now group condemnation leaves recruits full of self-doubt, guilt, and anxiety. Through this kind of manipulation, they are convinced that they can be saved only if they stay within the group.

Eventually, they no longer call or write to their families and friends. They may drop out of school or subordinate school to cult activities and end up unable to attend classes because cult activities occupy so much time. They may quit their jobs or go about them in a humdrum, distracted manner, losing all interest in prior careers or life goals. If elderly, they drop contact with family, friends, and neighbors and exhibit sudden changes of interest. It should be noted, however, that some of the more recent cults, in particular those espousing self-improvement or prosperity philosophies, tend to keep members busy working at their regular jobs and even taking on more than one job, so that they can earn more money to buy courses of various kinds from the cult.

CULT CONVERSION IS EXAGGERATED

James D. Tabor and Eugene V. Gallagher

James D. Tabor and Eugene V. Gallagher are the authors of Why
Waco? Cults and the Battle for Religious Freedom in America, *which
addresses America's intolerance and hostility toward cults and
alternative religions. In the following excerpt from their book,
Tabor and Gallagher describe how opponents of cults depict a
process of conversion to which no one is immune. According to
the authors, these opponents typically maintain that powerful cult
leaders use sophisticated brainwashing techniques to completely
dominate their zombie-like followers. This charge is ludicrous, the
authors contend, because it vastly overestimates the power of cult
leaders. Rather, they write, most people who come into contact
with cult leaders are easily able to resist conversion efforts.*

Since the mid-1980s, led by the efforts of the Cult Awareness Network
(CAN), various loosely related groups and individuals have worked
hard to stigmatize many new or alternative religious movements.
Those groups branded "cults" are portrayed as pervasively negative
influences in American society, particularly on unsuspecting adolescents and young adults, and, more recently, on senior citizens. As a
CAN brochure puts it, "A serious problem exists in our society as a
result of the emergence of groups, popularly called 'cults,' using mind
control (undue influence) and unethical means to recruit and retain
followers. Association with these groups can be harmful to followers
and disruptive to families, friends and society.". . . Psychiatrist Robert
J. Lifton's *Thought Reform and the Psychology of Totalism* has become a
canonical text for "cult" opponents. Its discussion of brainwashing in
China has provided a keystone in their argument that certain religious groups exercise undue influence over their members through a
process of "mind control.". . .

Since cultbusters frequently argue that "cult" leaders demonstrate
their extraordinary power by coercing conversions, it is worth examining that process in greater detail.

Though the cultbusters' understanding of religious conversion may
appear to have advanced in sophistication beyond the audacious

claim by Ted Patrick (an originator of the deprogramming process) that "cult" recruiters practice "on-the-spot hypnosis," the hallmark of their position remains the universal vulnerability to "cults." To the question "Who is vulnerable?" a CAN flyer answers, "Everyone—often those who believe they are too intelligent or strongwilled to be recruited." Another piece from CAN asserts that "anyone—*even you*—can be deceived." If true, those assertions would seem to doom CAN's efforts at public education since apparently no amount of education or self-awareness is sufficient to immunize anyone against the lure of "cults." But even if CAN's statements are taken as argumentative hyperbole, they still can be called into question. The underlying image of conversion as the result of an irresistible attraction exerted by surpassingly powerful "cult" leaders has no empirical basis. Statistical data simply do not indicate that a significant percentage of Americans have succumbed to the enticements of new and unconventional religions. In fact, simple observation shows that the number of American citizens actually involved in new or unconventional religious groups is quite small. (It is simply impossible to canvas those who may, at some time, have entertained or actually held an unconventional religious idea.) If, as the anticultists assert, anyone can be deceived, relatively few actually have been. The large-scale effects of the "cult" problem have simply not materialized. After all, at the height of its popularity the residents of the Mount Carmel center [home of David Koresh and the Branch Davidians] numbered barely over a hundred, and many of them were foreign nationals. Similarly, the population of the Peoples Temple Agricultural Mission in Jonestown, Guyana [home of Jim Jones and his followers], was around a thousand. In the light of those numbers, the alarm expressed by the anticult activists seems out of proportion to the number of people involved. Also, social-scientific research on conversion to new religious movements has shown that the vast majority of those who encounter such groups are eminently capable of resisting their attraction.

Universal Susceptibility to Cults

For the anticult activists everyone is a potential convert. One reason for that universal susceptibility is the great power attributed to "cult" leaders, who serve as powerful magnets. Anyone coming within its field of attraction will inexorably be pulled into the tightest possible relationship with the wily and alluring leader and will be converted. The convert's own intentions, convictions, or commitments have little or no role to play in such a scenario; whether the initial contact is intentional or accidental, the outcome is the same. Such a view of a passive self at the mercy of vastly superior forces has much in common with both theological and demonological images of the conversion process; the only difference lies in the nature of the superior forces in question. Most often in contemporary anticult arguments, the external forces are identified as psychological; the overwhelming personality of the leader through a process of brainwashing, mind control, or coercive persuasion generates the power that produces conversion. Whatever these forces, the explanations share a common structure. In each case, the convert is taken over by a power outside the individual's control, which essentially replaces his or her will and directs all subsequent activity. It is difficult to square such a portrait of conversion with the tiny number of people who actually become members of new or unconventional religious groups. Few authors have made that point as effectively as Eileen Barker in her seminal study *The Making of a Moonie: Choice or Brainwashing?* Barker's is one of the few examinations of the process of conversion to new or unconventional religious groups to incorporate trustworthy statistical evidence. In her quest to determine the validity of the brainwashing hypothesis to explain membership in the Unification Church in Great Britain, Barker conducted an extensive survey of people whose contact with the church included at least a visit to one of its centers. Barker's research offers no support whatsoever to the notion that "cult" leaders exercise an irresistible magnetism on potential converts. She summarizes her findings in this way: "If we start our calculations from the number of those who get as far as visiting an Unification centre, a generous estimate suggests that no more than 0.5 per cent will be associated with the movement two years later, and by no means all of these will be full-time members. In other words, it is just not true that anyone can be brainwashed by Unification techniques." The anticult activists' contention that all "cults" are alike gives Barker's conclusions even more force than she herself claims. But even if important differences between the Unification Church and the Mount Carmel community are granted, Barker's finding that only one person in two hundred who come into direct contact with the "Moonies" proves susceptible to their blandishments raises serious doubts about the magnetic theory of conversion to "cults."

As with their characterization of "cult" leaders, the anticult activists' depiction of the process of conversion turns out to be a flagrant oversimplification of a complicated social process. It vastly overestimates the power of leaders as it simultaneously reduces all participants in "cults" to interchangeable, faceless nobodies. Such reduction can be an effective polemical tool because it brushes aside any potential complications by making diverse evidence about individuals' contact with "cults" appear homogeneous. But it does not stand up to extended scrutiny. There are significant constraints on the power that any leader can successfully wield, and that which they do exercise is in many ways bestowed on them by their followers; similarly, their adherents are able to influence their own situations. Those who come into contact with "cult" leaders frequently have, can, and will reject both the messenger and the message.

TECHNIQUES FOR THOUGHT REFORM

Madeleine Landau Tobias and Janja Lalich

Madeleine Landau Tobias and Janja Lalich are the authors of *Captive Hearts, Captive Minds: Freedom and Recovery from Cults and Abusive Relationships*, from which the following essay is excerpted. Lalich is also a former cult member who works to expose cults' methods of recruitment. Tobias and Lalich argue that cults routinely subject members to systematic thought-reform techniques in order to elicit complete dependence on the group. These techniques, they explain, include isolating recruits from their families and the outside world, weakening them through inadequate diet and sleep deprivation, and convincing them that their very survival depends on compliance with the group. The end result, the authors charge, is a psychologically debilitated and rigidly obedient convert.

When we use the term *cult conversion,* we refer to the psychological and personality changes that a person undergoes as a result of being subjected to thought-reform and personality techniques, or a deliberate program of exploitative persuasion and behavior control. The effects of cult conversion are often disturbingly apparent to a cult member's family and friends, who may observe radical changes in the personality and behavior of their loved one. After recruitment into a cult or cultic relationship, people tend to withdraw, hold new beliefs and values, and behave in a manner quite different from, if not exactly the opposite of, their lifelong patterns.

Thought Reform

Many former cult members selectively deny aspects of their cult experience. Some become angry and resistant at the mention of mind control, thought reform, or brainwashing, thinking that these things could not possibly have been done to them. It is very threatening to a person's sense of self to contemplate having been controlled or taken over. The terms themselves—mind control, thought reform—sound harsh and unreal. Yet only by confronting the reality of psychological manipulation can ex-cult members overcome its effects.

Deceptive psychological and social manipulation are part and parcel of the cult experience. Over the years various labels have been used to describe this systematic process. Psychologist Robert Jay Lifton first used the term *thought reform* in the 1950s to describe the behavioral change processes he observed and studied in students at revolutionary universities in Communist China and in prisoners of war during the Korean War. Like many others in this field we dislike the term *brainwashing* because it is a buzzword, often associated with Communism or torture. A prison cell or a torture chamber is a far cry from the subtlety and sophistication of the techniques of manipulation and control found in today's cults. Therefore, we prefer the terms *thought reform* and *mind control*. . . .

Cult Conversion

The researchers who first studied the use of thought reform by the Chinese Communists witnessed a drastic conversion of belief, which they determined to be the result of what they called the "DDD syndrome"—debility, dependency, and dread. Robert Lifton and other researchers later demonstrated that debility, or actual physical coercion, was not a necessary ingredient for conversion. More recently psychologist Michael Langone proposed a modified DDD syndrome used in cult conversion: deception, dependency, dread.

Deception

Modern-day cults rely on subtle means of persuasion. The hallmark of a cult is its use of deception in the recruitment process and throughout membership. Rarely are the true purpose, beliefs, and ultimate goals of the group spelled out. Cults use meditation classes, computer schools, health clinics, telemarketing programs, publishing enterprises, financial appeals, business seminars, real estate ventures, Bible study groups, political study groups, and campus activity groups as front organizations to lure potential new members into the recruitment web.

Because cults appeal to the normal desires of ordinary people, cult recruitment may be viewed as a kind of courtship. The prospective devotee is wooed with the promise of reward, be it personal fulfillment, special knowledge, spiritual growth, political satisfaction, religious salvation, lifelong companionship, riches, power—whatever is most dear to that person at the time. This connection to a person's innermost desire is the recruitment "hook." In a way, the cult leader becomes like a genie holding out the promise of wish fulfillment. Most often, the deception takes root during this initial phase of recruitment.

Dependency

The recruitment stage and the early days of membership are often called the "honeymoon phase." Frequently, as a teaser, one of the recruit's wishes may be granted. Once such a favor is granted, the potential recruit is made to feel even more indebted to the group, wishing to return the favor.

Meanwhile, recruits and new members are encouraged to share or confess their deepest secrets, weaknesses, and fears, opening themselves up as the cult leadership probes for further knowledge. Prospective disciples are carefully paced throughout the conversion process. They are fed just enough information to maintain their interest; they are tricked and psychologically coerced (usually via guilt or fear) into making further commitments to the group or relationship; they are never pushed so far as to cause undue discomfort or outright suspicion.

To cultivate dependency, long-term members model preferred group behavior that brings reward, status, and acceptance. This provides social proof of the efficacy, strengths, and advantages of the new belief system. The superiority of the group is firmly established through the combination of peer pressure and constant reminders of the new member's weaknesses and vulnerabilities. The new member begins to rely on the beliefs of the group or leader for his or her future well-being. Having been successful in capturing the interest of the recruit, the group can now lead the person into desired frames of thought and types of behavior that meet the cult's needs and goals.

At this point psychological coercion also increases, with the intensified use of meditation, chanting, long prayer sessions, hypnosis, sleep deprivation, and other mind-altering techniques of manipulation and control. At the same time indoctrination into the "sacred science" continues with long study sessions, lectures, and seminars. Encouraged to declare formal allegiance to the group or "path" while becoming increasingly isolated from former ways of thinking, the new member now accepts the group's definition of what is right and wrong, good and bad, and converts to the cause.

The cult now puts forth even higher expectations and demands. The new member's weaknesses and failures are emphasized and criticized more and more, with little focus on strengths. Nothing short of total dedication is accepted. The group or leader is presented as always right. Doubts and dissent are actively discouraged, if not punished.

To suppress the recruit's "evil" or precult personality, increased participation in group activities and even more practice of mind-altering techniques are actively promoted by the group. Either because it is forbidden by the group or because it is an act of self-protection, access to outside information is limited and the new member is discouraged from maintaining precult contacts, especially with family. Such contact might point up the conflicts between new and old beliefs and upset the still delicate underpinning necessary to secure adherence to the group.

Dread

Gradually the cult insinuates a feeling of dread in the recruit's mind, which further isolates the members and prevents defections from the group. This is accomplished by increasing dependency on the group through escalated demands, intensified criticism and humiliation, and, in some cults, subtle or overt threats of punishment which may be physical, spiritual, emotional, or sexual. Even infants and children may be held responsible for the smallest infractions, forced to conform to group demands despite their age. Threats of excommunication, shunning, and abandonment by the group become powerful forces of control once members become fully dependent on the group and alienated from their former support network. If a person is completely estranged from the rest of the world, staying put appears the only option. Members come to dread losing what they consider to be the group's psychological support, regardless of how controlling or debilitating that support may be in reality.

Another technique used to invoke dread is the induction of phobias. Cults convey phobic messages, for example: "If you leave, you are doomed to countless cycles of incarnation." "You will go crazy or die if you leave the group." "You will be ruined and never find a way to survive." "You are doomed to failure or terrible accidents if you do not obey." "If you leave this church, you are leaving God." Almost all groups use this sort of phobia induction as a means of control and domination.

The Double Bind

In addition to the techniques described above, the double bind may be used to enhance the effectiveness of the thought-reform program. This emotional cul-de-sac is defined in *Webster's Ninth New Collegiate Dictionary* as a "psychological dilemma in which a usually dependent person receives conflicting interpersonal communication from a single source or *faces disparagement no matter what his response to a situation*" [emphasis ours]. It imparts a message of hopelessness: you're damned if you do and damned if you don't.

Cult manipulations are typically designed to elicit compliance. They demand and have an answer. The double bind, however, has no answer. The person is criticized no matter what he or she does. Jackson's [the name has been changed] story provides an example:

> Jackson was in a left-wing political cult that taught its members "to take initiative within the bounds of discipline," which was supposed to mean that members were to apply all their creativity and intelligence to whatever situation they were in without violating the group's strict norms and policies. This rule allowed the leadership to criticize members all the time because just about any independent behavior could

be deemed "outside" the bounds of the discipline, while at the same time to not act in any given situation could be criticized as "wimpishness, cowardice, or passivity."

While at a demonstration in front of City Hall protesting a cut in city workers' wages, Jackson saw the mayor approaching. Thinking himself a brave militant ready to defend his organization's stand, Jackson walked directly up to the mayor and asked him what he was going to do about the wage cuts. When this action was reported to the cult leader, she blew up and ordered Jackson to be harshly criticized for breaking discipline, saying that Jackson was self-centered, only promoting himself and trying to grab power. One week later Jackson was sent to another picket line, where a union boss was expected to show up. The leader told Jackson that he better be prepared to confront the union boss. "What about?" Jackson asked, trembling. "You know damn well what about!" exclaimed his leader.

Double binds magnify dependence by injecting an additional element of unpredictability into cult members' relationships to their leadership. Consequently, members can never become too comfortable. Fear prevents them from challenging those on whom they have become dependent. When this tactic is successful, members are unable to move out of a state of dependence. The mere fact of living creates insecurity and induces fear and withdrawal.

When this type of manipulation (a blatant power trip) is used, cult members spend most of their time feeling as though they are walking on eggs, knowing that they must act—and yet to act may bring rebuke, punishment, or worse.

The Cult "Pseudopersonality"

Two leading cult experts, Margaret Singer and Louis Jolyon West, professor of psychiatry at the University of California at Los Angeles (UCLA) Neuropsychiatric Institute, developed the following list of elements that are most likely to be part of a successful cult indoctrination. Each element is a drastic technique used to control and exploit the individual.

1. Isolation of the recruit and manipulation of his environment
2. Control over channels of communication and information
3. Debilitation through inadequate diet and fatigue
4. Degradation or diminution of the self
5. Induction of uncertainty, fear, and confusion, with joy and certainty through surrender to the group as the goal
6. Alternation of harshness and leniency in a context of discipline
7. Peer pressure, often applied through ritualized struggle sessions, generating guilt and requiring open confessions

8. Insistence by seemingly all-powerful hosts that the recruit's survival—physical or spiritual—depends on identifying with the group

9. Assignment of monotonous tasks or repetitive activities, such as chanting or copying written materials

10. Acts of symbolic betrayal and renunciation of self, family, and previously held values, designed to increase the psychological distance between the recruit and his previous way of life

The effects of such a program, according to Singer and West, are that "as time passes, the member's psychological condition may deteriorate. He becomes incapable of complex, rational thought; his responses to questions become stereotyped; he finds it difficult to make even simple decisions unaided; his judgment about events in the outside world is impaired. At the same time, there may be such a reduction of insight that he fails to realize how much he has changed."

Michael Langone summarizes the effects of the conversion process this way: "After converts commit themselves to a cult, the cult's way of thinking, feeling, and acting becomes second nature, while important aspects of their precult personalities are suppressed or, in a sense, decay through disuse. . . . If allowed to break into consciousness, suppressed memories or nagging doubts may generate anxiety which, in turn, may trigger a defensive trance-induction, such as speaking in tongues, to protect the cult-imposed system of thoughts, feelings, and behavior. Such persons may function adequately—at least on a superficial level. Nevertheless, their continued adjustment depends upon their keeping their old thinking styles, goals, values, and personal attachments in storage."

Upon leaving a cult, ex-members are bequeathed an altered version of themselves. This is why recently exited cult members often appear confused, at a loss for what to say or do. Cult membership tends to reduce formerly well-adjusted and intelligent individuals to slow thinkers who must try to make their way back to what they vaguely remember being like before joining the group. Often they lack self-confidence and are riddled with shame, guilt, and fear. Many former members state that they weren't able to really laugh or cry for months after leaving the group. They felt unable to connect with people, afraid to say something "wrong" or "stupid." At the time, many didn't even realize how they were behaving or reacting.

A dramatic change of identity is required in order for the mind to adapt to a high level of coercive deception. This phenomenon has been identified by Robert Lifton as *doubling*. Doubling is the formation of a second self which lives side by side with the former one, often for a considerable time. According to Lifton, doubling is a universal phenomenon reflecting each person's capacity for the "divided self," or opposing tendencies in the self. "But," he writes, "that 'opposing self' can become dangerously unrestrained, as it did in the Nazi doctors.

. . . That opposing self can become the usurper from within and replace the original self until it 'speaks' for the entire person."

During cult recruitment and throughout membership, the devotee is encouraged to lose his or her personal identity and become absorbed in the persona of the group or leader. In some Eastern meditation cults this is linked to the metaphor of dyeing one's robes over and over again until they are the same color as the guru's: by emulating the guru, meditating, and copying his behavior, one eventually becomes one with the Master. In other cults this oneness or state of totalism is achieved through other types of training and conditioning. The mind-manipulating techniques used to induce altered states also serve to support the development and emergence of the cult personality.

Thus we see that under the stress of complying with the cult's demands, the individual member develops a secondary cult personality. This emergence of a "pseudopersonality," as it is called by psychologist Louis J. West, enables a person to carry out cult-imposed activities that would normally be against his or her value system, such as begging, sexual promiscuity, lying, forgoing needed medical attention, and participating in violence or criminal activity. This phenomenon helps to explain why there is no apparent internal disagreement between the competing value systems of a person's cult and precult personalities. The former smiles benignly because the latter is safely bound and gagged, locked up in a cage of fear. Simply put, it explains why decent and rational people can end up doing indecent and irrational things.

This capacity to adapt has also been recognized as integral to the human psyche. At times it can save lives, such as for a soldier in combat. This life-saving aspect is relevant to our understanding of the cult member's situation, wherein personality adaptation is both a cult-imposed requirement and a person's means of survival.

As explained earlier, the goal of thought reform is for the subject to become one with the ideal. In cults, personal ego boundaries disappear as the member begins to live for the group or the ideology. This change in identification, often accompanied by such actions as leaving school, changing jobs, dropping old friends, interests, and hobbies, and avoiding family, is what so alarms people as they watch a family member or friend become totally consumed by cult life.

Many who come out of cultic situations may not even be aware that they have taken on a pseudopersonality and, along with their families and friends, are puzzled by their own inconsistent behaviors and feelings. This may cause some former members to feel even more isolated and frustrated, because they feel and know that something is awfully wrong but do not know what or how. Obviously, prospective cult members are not informed during recruitment that such deep, devastating changes might occur.

THE EFFECTIVENESS OF MIND CONTROL TECHNIQUES IS EXAGGERATED

Bob and Gretchen Passantino

Bob and Gretchen Passantino direct Answers in Action, a non-profit religious organization that promotes a Christian world-view. They also write extensively on cults, including the books *Answers to the Cultist at Your Door* and *Witch Hunt*. In the following selection, the Passantinos refute the assumptions that cults successfully employ mind control techniques to convert members and that all individuals are susceptible to these techniques. Although the authors concede that cults may indeed use psychological pressure or other deplorable tactics in their recruiting efforts, they assert that there is no evidence that these methods rob individuals of personal responsibility or the ability to think critically. To make their point, the Passantinos outline commonly accepted theories about mind control techniques supposedly used by cults and then present arguments that contradict each assumption. The authors conclude that mind control theories are grossly overstated and that cult members are morally responsible for their decision to join a cult.

For many people, especially secular cult observers, the theory of mind control is used to explain [how people could pledge their lives to bizarre, exclusivistic religious movements]. The cult mind control model is so commonly raised in explanation that many people assume its validity without question.

In this article, we look behind the assumptions of the mind control model and uncover the startling reality that "cult mind control" is, at best, a distorted misnomer for cult conversion that robs individuals of personal moral responsibility. While mind control model advocates rightly point out that cults often practice deception, emotional manipulation, and other unsavory recruitment tactics, we believe a critical, well-reasoned examination of the evidence disproves the cult

Excerpted from Bob and Gretchen Passantino, "Overcoming the Bondage of Victimization" (1994), www.answers.org/CultsAndReligions/mind_control.html. Reprinted by permission of the authors. *References in the original have been omitted in this reprint.*

mind control model and instead affirms the importance of informed, biblically based religious commitment.

Assumptions of Mind Control

The theory of cult mind control is part of a contemporary adversarial approach to many cults, new religious movements, and non-traditional churches. In this approach sociological and psychological terminology has been substituted for Christian terminology. Cult involvement is no longer described as religious conversion, but as mind control induction. Cult membership is not characterized as misplaced religious zeal but as programming. And the cultist who leaves his group is no longer described as redeemed, but as returned to a neutral religious position. And rather than evangelism of cult members, we now have "intervention counseling."

And biblical apologetics has been replaced by cognitive dissonance techniques. A parent's plea has changed from "How can my adult child be saved?" to "How can my adult child revert to his/her pre-cult personality?" Biblical analysis and evangelism of the cults has become overshadowed by allegedly "value neutral" social science descriptions and therapy-oriented counseling.

The principal assumptions of the cult mind control model can be summarized under eight categories:

1. Cults' ability to control the mind supersedes that of the best military "brainwashers."
2. Cult recruits become unable to think or make decisions for themselves.
3. Cult recruits assume "cult" personalities and subsume their core personalities.
4. Cultists cannot decide to leave their cults.
5. A successful intervention must break the mind control, find the core personality, and return the individual to his/her pre-cult status.
6. Psychology and sociology are used to explain cult recruitment, membership, and disaffection.
7. Religious conversion and commitment may be termed "mind control" if it meets certain psychological and sociological criteria, regardless of its doctrinal or theological standards.
8. The psychological and sociological standards which define mind control are not absolute, but fall in a relative, subjective continuum from "acceptable" social and/or religious affiliation to "unacceptable."

According to most cult mind control model advocates, no one is immune to the right mind control tactics used at the right time. Anyone is susceptible. For example, Steven Hassan, recognized as a premier source for the cult mind control model, writes in his book, *Combatting Cult Mind Control*, "Anyone, regardless of family background, can be recruited into a cult. The major variable is not the person's family but the cult recruiter's level of skill." Dr. Paul Martin, evangelical director of a rehabilitation center for former cultists, writes, "But the truth of the matter is, virtually anyone can get involved in a cult under the right circumstances. . . . Regardless of one's spiritual or psychological health, whether one is weak or strong, cultic involvement can happen to anyone."

Evangelical exit counselor Craig Branch told us in an interview that, even though he was extremely knowledgeable and experienced regarding cult mind control, he still could be caught by cult mind control administered at the right time by the right person.

The cult mind control model is based on a fundamental conviction that the cultist becomes unable to make responsible and rational choices or decisions (particularly the choice to leave the group), and that psychological techniques are the most effective ways to free them to make decisions once more. This foundation is non-negotiable to the mind control model, and is at the root of what we consider so flawed about the mind control concept. . . .

Personal Responsibility

Those holding to the mind control model have made the generalization that most cults have internal social pressures and religious practices which, if not identical in nature, are similar in effect; and that average cult members are similarly affected by these teachings, techniques, and practices. We reject this generalization, though we will grant—and in fact have stated publicly—that many cults have made deceptive claims, used faulty logic, misrepresented their beliefs, burdened their followers with unscriptural feelings of guilt, and sought to bring people into financial or moral compromise to unethical demands. Yet it does not necessarily or automatically follow that these pressures, practices, or demands remove an individual's personal responsibility for his or her actions.

The cult mind control model assumes that a combination of pressure and deception necessarily disables personal responsibility. Exit counselor Hassan recognizes that the cult mind control model (which he has adopted) is incompatible with the traditional philosophical and Christian view of man as a responsible moral agent:

> First of all, accepting that unethical mind control can affect anybody challenges the age-old philosophical notion (the one on which our current laws are based) that man is a rational being, responsible for, and in control of, his every action. Such a world view does not allow for any concept of mind control.

The Brainwashing Evidence

. . . Neither brainwashing, mind control's supposed precursor, nor mind control itself, have any appreciable demonstrated effectiveness.

Psychologist Margaret Singer and other mind control model propo-
nents are not always candid about this fact: The early brainwashing
attempts were largely unsuccessful. Even though the Koreans and Chinese used extreme forms of physical coercion as well as persuasive
coercion [in brainwashing attempts in the 1950s among American
prisoners of war], very few individuals subjected to their techniques
changed their basic world views or commitments.

The CIA also experimented with brainwashing. Though not using
Korean or Chinese techniques of torture, beatings, and group dynamics, the CIA did experiment with drugs (including LSD) and medical
therapies such as electroshock in their research on mind control.
Their experiments failed to produce even one potential Manchurian
Candidate [a successfully brainwashed individual], and the program
was finally abandoned.

Although some mind control model advocates bring up studies
that appear to provide objective data in support of their theories, such
is not the case. These studies are generally flawed in several areas: (1)
Frequently the respondents are not from a wide cross-section of ex-
members but disproportionately are those who have been exit-
counseled by mind control model advocates who tell them they were
under mind control; (2) Frequently the sample group is so small its
results cannot be fairly representative of cult membership in general;
(3) It is almost impossible to gather data from the same individuals
before cult affiliation, during cult affiliation, and after cult disaffection, so respondents are sometimes asked to answer as though they
were not yet members, or as though they were still members, etc.
Each of these flaws introduces unpredicatiblity and subjectivity that
make such study results unreliable.

Low Recruitment Rates

The evidence against the effectiveness of mind control techniques is
even more overwhelming. Studies show that the vast majority of
young people approached by new religious movements (NRMs) never
join despite heavy recruitment tactics. This low rate of recruitment
provides ample evidence that whatever techniques of purported mind
control are used as cult recruiting tools, they do not work on most
people. Even of those interested enough to attend a recruitment seminar or weekend, the majority do not join the group. Author and
researcher Eileen Barker documents that out of 1000 people persuaded
by the Moonies to attend one of their overnight programs in 1979,
90% had no further involvement. Only 8% joined for more than one
week, and less than 4% remained members in 1981, two years later:

> . . . and, with the passage of time, the number of continuing
> members who joined in 1979 has continued to fall. If the cal-
> culation were to start from those who, for one reason or

another, had visited one of the movement's centres in 1979, at least 999 out of every 1,000 of those people had, by the mid-1980s, succeeded in resisting the persuasive techniques of the Unification Church.

Of particular importance is that this extremely low rate of conversion is known even to Hassan, the best-known mind control model advocate whose book is the standard text for introducing concerned parents to mind control/exit counseling. In his personal testimony of his own involvement with the Unification Church, he notes that he was the first convert to join at the center in Queens; that during the first three months of his membership he only recruited two more people; and that pressure to recruit new members was only to reach the goal of one new person per member per month, a surprisingly low figure if we are to accept the inevitable success of cult mind control techniques.

Additionally, natural attrition (people leaving the group without specific intervention) was much higher than the self-claimed 65% deprogramming success figure! It is far more likely a new convert would leave the cult within the first year of his membership than it is that he would become a long term member.

This data, confirming low rates of conversion and high rates of disaffection, is deadly to the mind control model. The data reveals that the theory of cult mind control is not confirmed by the statistical evidence. . . .

As Barker summarizes, "far more people have left the very NRMs from which people are most commonly deprogrammed than have stayed in them, and the overwhelming majority of these people have managed to leave without the need for any physical coercion.". . .

Creating Victims

Many people who join cults want to help the needy, forsake materialism, or develop personal independence from their families; not necessarily bad goals, although misguided by false cult teachings. The cult mind control model, however, attributes cult membership primarily to mind control and thereby denigrates or discounts such positive activities and goals, misaffiliated to cults as they are.

The mind control model also fails to give proper weight to the role natural suggestibility plays in making one vulnerable to the cults. Highly suggestible people are especially susceptible to religious salesmanship as well as many other "sales pitches."

The cult mind control model instead focuses on victimization, that a cult member joins as a result of mind control and not as the result of personal choice. Adopting a "victimization" perspective actually strips the cult member of his capacity for rational activity. The cult mind control model epitomizes a "victim" mentality. Hassan explains his approach to counseling a cult member:

First, I demonstrate to him that he is in a trap—a situation
where he is psychologically disabled and can't get out. Second, I show him that he didn't originally choose to enter a
trap. Third, I point out that other people in other groups are
in similar traps. Fourth, I tell him that it is possible to get out
of the trap.

This kind of victimization is very popular in our society today,
although it has not demonstrated any evidential validity nor any ability to set the foundation for emotional or mental health.

Problems with the cult victimization idea can be illustrated by
looking at other areas outside the new religious movements. We have
the John Bradshaw "model" of adults as "inner children" who never
grew up because of their "dysfunctional" families. We have the many
twelve-step spawned derivative groups where members seem to focus
more on their powerlessness against whatever addictive "illness" they
have than on another twelve-step maxim: personal responsibility.
And we have the many "Adult Children" support groups where members uncover the sources of all their problems—dysfunctional parents.

One of the most visible applications of the mind control model
today is in the area of repressed memories of early childhood abuse
(of satanic ritual abuse, simple child abuse, alien or UFO abduction,
past lives, etc.). Amazingly, the mind control model is used to
describe two contrasting portions of this problem. First, therapists
and clients who believe they have uncovered previously repressed
memories of early childhood abuse believe that the original abusers
practice mind control on their victims. One of the most extreme
examples of this is psychologist Corry Hammond, who postulates a
sophisticated system of mind control he believes was developed from
experimental Nazi systems.

Second, falsely accused parents and other family members often
believe the mind control model, applied to the relationship between
the therapist and the accusing client, explains how adult children
could sincerely believe and accuse their own fathers, mothers, brothers, uncles, and grandparents of performing unspeakable horrors on
them as children, including human sacrifice, rape, incest, mutilation,
etc. Many times these adult children have publicly denounced their
parents and refused any contact with them for years. Surely to believe
such outrageous fictions, they must be under therapeutic mind control! Finally, once adult "survivors" come to the realization that their
memories are false, they must deal with the reality that they have
accused their loved ones of horrible atrocities. One alleged survivor,
struggling to maintain belief in her alleged recovered memories,
acknowledged this painful responsibility:

I wish I could say that I knew [my memories] were 100 percent true. But I can't. If they are all based on falsehoods, I

deserve to be damned, and that is really tough. I've made some really important decisions that have affected a lot of people. I still get back to [the feeling that] the essence of the belief has to be true.

How could they have ever caused their families such anguish? They must have been victims of therapeutic mind control!

And yet, such a view fosters a crippling victimization that says, in effect, "you couldn't do anything to prevent this insidious mind control" and, consequently, what could you possibly do to protect yourself or your loved ones in the future?

Speaking about cults, Barker makes this clear, saying,

> Those who leave by themselves may have concluded that they made a mistake and that they recognized that fact and, as a result, they did something about it: they left. Those who have been deprogrammed, on the other hand, are taught that it was not they who were responsible for joining; they were the victims of mind-control techniques—and these prevented them from leaving. Research has shown that, unlike those who have been deprogrammed (and thereby taught that they had been brainwashed), those who leave voluntarily are extremely unlikely to believe that they were ever the victims of mind control.

An improper victimization model, whether used to understand cult recruitment, repressed memories, adult emotional distress, or false accusations of abuse, does not provide the education, critical thinking apparatus, or coping mechanisms necessary to protect oneself from further victimization, and, most importantly, such theories do not focus on the life-transforming gospel as the ultimate solution.

Additionally, true victims, such as small children, victims of rape, robbery, or murder, those who truly are unable to predict or prevent their victimization, have their predicament cheapened and obscured by those who are not truly defenseless victims.

This model has become standard for many evangelical Christians who have therapists, attribute their current problems to "dysfunctional" relationships, and trace their personal inadequacies to emotionally harmful childhoods (everyone's a dysfunctional "adult child" of alcoholism, or abuse, or isolationism, or authoritarianism). Everyone is a victim. One doesn't need to be saved from one's own sins as much as from the sins of others. Psychology and sociology have replaced Scripture for understanding human behavior and developing emotionally and spiritually healthy persons. Yet nowhere in Scripture do we find support for the idea complaint first voiced by Eve that "the devil—or the cult leader—made me do it." One cannot remove human responsibility without also destroying human morality. . . .

Theological Inconsistencies

If the cult recruiter's skill at manipulation is considered so coercive that members are not responsible for their own beliefs, actions, or even the decision to join/stay in the cult, then many biblical affirmations about personal responsibility and decision-making are jeopardized. To a secular mind control model advocate, this may seem a trivial objection. But several advocates are Christian evangelicals and must come to terms with the theological inconsistencies introduced when the cult mind control model is adopted.

For example, in the Garden, Satan personally appeared to orchestrate the temptation of Eve—and who could be more persuasive? Our first parents succumbed to the temptation and were cast out of the Garden, and all of humanity thereafter have been penalized by this primal sin. If our first parents could be held morally responsible when confronted by the Ultimate Tempter, how is it that we seek to excuse ourselves or our offspring when confronted by human tempters of far less power, skill, and charisma?

Moreover, we observe that both Adam and Eve were penalized alike, even though the temptation was very well different for each. Eve's temptation was mediated by the direct approach of Satan; Adam's temptation occurred via his wife, and we are not told that Satan appeared to Adam as he did to Eve. Yet, regardless of whether Satan's presence was immediate or remote, firsthand or secondhand, both shared ethical culpability for their action.

It is also instructive to note that the second sin of Adam and Eve was blameshifting, the attempt to elude personal responsibility. Eve blamed the Serpent, and Adam blamed Eve. Though God loved them deeply, He did not accept this rationalization then, and He will not accept similar excuses made today for our own wrong beliefs and behavior.

This carefully focused evaluation has shown that the Bogey Man of cult mind control is nothing but a ghost story, good for inducing an adrenaline high and maintaining a crusade, but irrelevant to reality. The reality is that people who have very real spiritual, emotional, and social needs are looking for fulfillment and significance for their lives. Ill-equipped to test the false gospels of this world, they make poor decisions about their religious affiliations. Poor decisions, yes, but decisions for which they are personally responsible nonetheless.

As Christians who believe in an absolute standard of truth and religious reality, we cannot ignore the spiritual threat of the cults. We must promote critical thinking, responsible education, biblical apologetics, and Christian evangelism. We must recognize that those who join the cults, while morally responsible, are also spiritually ignorant. The power of the gospel (Romans 1:16) erases spiritual ignorance and provides the best opportunity possible for right moral and religious choices. "So if the Son sets you free, you will be free indeed" (John 8:36).

CULTS AND DEFENSIVE BELIEF SYSTEMS

Dr. Arthur Janov

Children need to be loved, protected, and made to feel safe, according to Dr. Arthur Janov. When parents or other caregivers do not meet these essential needs, writes Dr. Janov, children repress the debilitating pain of feeling unloved below the level of conscious awareness. However, he states, these repressed emotions continue to exert their influence into adulthood, and individuals may develop defensive belief systems in response to these driving needs. Cults are particularly attractive for such individuals since through membership they can experience the approval and acceptance they missed during childhood, he explains. This is why, Dr. Janov concludes, people who crave love will remain vulnerable to recruitment by cults or similar movements, even when membership in such groups defies logic. Dr. Janov is the author of *The New Primal Scream: Primal Therapy 20 Years On* and is the director of Dr. Arthur Janov's Primal Center in Venice, California.

The 1993 confrontation in Waco, Tex. [between followers of David Koresh—called Branch Davidians—and U.S. federal authorities], like the mass suicide in Jonestown in 1978, is the tragic outcome of predictable events.

There are key psychological factors that lead people into belief systems, cults and self destructive situations. Hundreds of followers of Jim Jones, at his behest, drank poison en masse, believing that they would meet later on in another form of Utopia. His belief system was strong enough to override the human instinct for survival.

At Jonestown as in Waco, deprived childhood need is the glue that attaches the followers to the leader and vice versa. The followers are in the grip of something much stronger and much older than their powers of judgment. They are being driven by a matrix of unconscious feelings and unending neediness that renders them as naive and vulnerable as an infant turning toward its mother for warmth, sustenance, protection and guidance.

Reprinted from Dr. Arthur Janov, "A Craving for Love, Cradle to Grave," *Los Angeles Times*, March 28, 1993, by permission of the author.

The Pain of Neglect

The needs I am referring to lie under the rubric of love. Children need to be touched, caressed and soothed. They need to be heard, protected and made to feel safe. They need parents who will allow them to express their feelings and who will help them with those feelings. When these needs go unmet early on, they turn into what I call Primal Pain. A child cries out from his crib for his mother. Instead of being attended to, he is met with angry eyes, a hostile voice and punishment for the "crime" of crying. He soon learns to put away his need. But it doesn't disappear; it is simply more pain than he can integrate. Repression rushes in to quell his feelings of need and make him feel more comfortable. He soon loses touch with his need, but the pain lingers on for a lifetime below the level of conscious awareness. In adult life, that unconscious need will be displaced onto others.

Can you imagine what it takes for a child to accept that he is not loved, that he never will be? That justice will never come, that it will never get any better? That all he has to look forward to is absolute nothingness, hopelessness and lovelessness for as long as he lives? We can see the pull of the belief system that defends against such feelings, and why brainwashing of all kinds works in the face of utter hopelessness.

The needy follower feeds on the leader, whose unfulfilled need is probably even more intense than that of the lowliest member of his flock. It is not an accident that many of the tyrants and demagogues of this world are typically products of broken, distorted childhoods, looking for fulfillment symbolically in the present.

The leader blots out the intolerable pains of his or her life through the control and manipulation of others; the follower finds relief through being controlled. A very stable symbiosis of mutually dependent parasites.

Defensive belief systems are welding devices. They weld members into a social unit so that they feel they belong. They can then share their private craziness with others. It is what I call socially validated insanity: My unreality is validated because many others believe it; and the more who believe, the more I am reassured and relieved not to be alone.

Hard-Wired Needs

All this is not so different from the urban gang phenomenon. Gangs are welding. The need for approval, to belong and to be protected is similar to that in a cult. You are not going to talk someone out of a gang or a cult, because you can't talk someone out of his needs. They are hard-wired.

Few followers tried to leave Jonestown or, in the beginning of the siege, the Branch Davidian compound, because to leave is to feel forsaken, to be faced again with the early catastrophic feelings of rejection and abandonment, which drove the person to join up in the first place.

One way that defensive belief systems come into being, even fairly early in a child's life, is through being taught not to express feelings, not to speak thoughts that are unacceptable, not to express resentment, jealousy or other negative thoughts, not to speak badly of others and never to say what is in one's heart. Once installed, this censoring process continues automatically. The child comes later on to substitute ideas for what he or she really feels. Having unreal ideas as an adult is just a logical extension of what happened in early childhood.

All of us are programmed to some extent to reject and deny the voice of our feelings. That is the function of belief systems: to quiet the feeling that there is no one to care, to protect and to love. The drug of beliefs anesthetizes a lifetime of deprivation. A threat to the belief system is met with desperation; the needy are prepared to do anything, even to kill or, as at Jonestown, to end their own lives, to avoid being left open to pain without a defender.

I am not referring to a drug metaphorically. We are able to manufacture a morphine equivalent in our brains called endorphin whose secretion can be influenced by ideas. Ideas can be like a shot of morphine, in that certain ideas are calming: "You are wonderful. You are special, God's gift," and so on. The ideas must run counter to the real feelings of hopelessness, feeling unimportant, worthless, of no value to anyone. Once someone offers ideas strong enough to counter what one lacked in childhood, one is "under the influence."

Instead of trying to feel the void that lurks inside the hidden crevices of the unconscious, the believer rises above hopelessness and helplessness into "salvation." What is he saved from? His feelings. Himself.

It is not a matter of what belief, but the fact of believing. The endorphins whip into action irrespective of the content of the belief so long as implied in it is hope and avoidance of death. Those chemicals do not distinguish among Buddha, Jesus, Jones or Koresh. They just do their job when called upon.

CHAPTER 3

CULTS AND SOCIETY

APOCALYPTIC CULTS

Paul Kaihla

Paul Kaihla asserts that doomsday cults are not a new phenomenon; rather, they have existed in society for two thousand years. In fact, he states, mainstream Christianity also contains the concept of the apocalypse, a frightening and violent time when civilization will come to an end. Apocalyptic cults thrive because the message of the apocalypse appeals to peoples' deep-seated anxieties about the future, the ultimate fate of the world, and the afterlife, he writes. Kaihla notes that these cults also flourish in societies that are experiencing economic chaos, political turmoil, or other types of instability. Thus, contends Kaihla, the lure of a messianic cult can be overwhelmingly strong: A cult's claim that its followers will survive the apocalypse and establish some type of heavenly kingdom offers a comforting message to those plagued by doomsday fears or societal unrest. Kaihla writes for *Maclean's*, a weekly Canadian news magazine.

In the final conflict, the sons of Light will send their armies against the sons of Darkness. The "battles of annihilation" will rage across the world for 40 years, at the end of which God "shall burn the sinners in an eternal blaze." That dreadful scenario is not the reckless scaremongering of a latter-day doomsday huckster or televangelist. The prophecy was in fact laid down 2,000 years ago by the Essenes, a messianic Jewish sect, in a series of leather manuscripts that became known as the Dead Sea Scrolls. The Essenes, who saw themselves as the world's final generation, had withdrawn into the desert to observe their strict beliefs, away from what they considered a corrupt society—and to train for the ultimate moment when the Messiah would appear. They would be the sole survivors of the apocalypse. The end did come, as predicted, but it was not the Essenes who triumphed. The religious fanatics' main retreat was destroyed in AD 68 by Roman soldiers conducting scorched-earth raids across Palestine to put down rebellion.

But the mysterious Essenes left behind a vision of the future that continues to haunt and engross people even in the video age. For the Dead Sea Scrolls contain the earliest written account of the central con-

Reprinted from Paul Kaihla, "A Deadly Tradition: Apocalyptic Cults Have Flourished in the West for Two Thousand Years," *Macleans*, October 17, 1994, by permission of *Macleans* magazine, Toronto, Canada.

cept of the biblical apocalypse—that civilization, and time itself, would come to a shuddering conclusion in a conflagration brought about by the wickedness of man. The Messiah's appearance would ultimately bathe the entire Earth in "the glory of the Lord." The 1994 collective suicide or murder of at least 53 followers of doomsday cult leader Luc Jouret demonstrated once again how, even today, fanatics are quite prepared to carry the themes of the apocalypse to tragic extremes.

The shocking saga of Jouret's sect will no doubt lead some commentators to conclude, ominously—as they did after the 1993 siege in Waco, Tex., and after the 1978 mass suicide–murder of 914 cultists led by Jim Jones in Jonestown, Guyana—that the deaths are yet another sign of moral crisis or the alienation of the modern age. But in fact, apocalyptic cults like Jouret's have been present since the day of the Essenes. And one reason they continue to prosper, psychiatrists and scholars say, is that the message of the apocalypse appeals to deep-seated anxieties in the human psyche. "Many people find the great imponderable questions of life unbearable," says Toronto psychiatrist Andrew Malcolm. "They need concrete, clear-cut answers to existential problems like what comes after death, and what is the fate of the world. There is no simpler solution than a messianic cult with a program where all followers will be saved and reassembled on the other side of time after the apocalypse."

Historians point to other factors. Cults flourish when a society experiences oppression or economic chaos, and people embrace militant Armageddon-style philosophies that promise a better life to come. Those conditions were certainly present when the Essenes fled to the desert in the second century BC. After three centuries of relative peace, the Jewish tribes had become the target of persecution under a series of tyrannical foreign rulers.

But tragic cults were by no means found only in ancient Palestine. In Europe, during the chaos of the early Reformation, a radical Protestant group known as Anabaptists seized control of the German town of Münster in an apocalyptic frenzy and proclaimed the New Jerusalem. A charismatic young tailor named Jan Bockelson took control in 1534, declared himself the new messiah and forced the town's women into polygamous marriages. Those who resisted were executed. The local Catholic bishop laid siege to Münster with the help of neighboring princes and cities. Unlike David Koresh and the Branch Davidians in Waco, the Münster Anabaptists surrendered—only to be slaughtered after they laid down their arms.

Like Bockelson's regime, later doomsday cults were also breakaway groups rebelling against established religions and local authorities. In North America, rapid industrialization helped to fuel such movements. Western New York state was a hotbed of cult activity in the first half of the 1800s, when the Erie Canal was built. In the inevitable backlash against the new moneyed class, dozens of sects sprang up.

They included the Mormons, who claimed that Jesus had visited America during his lifetime and would return there for the Second Coming, as well as the Millerites, who believed that the world would end on Oct. 22, 1844.

In fact, thousands of Millerites in Canada and the United States sold their possessions, dressed in robes and waited for the Second Coming on rooftops, hills and haystacks on the appointed day because they believed it would shorten their journey to heaven. In Oshawa, Ont., a Millerite named Sarah Terwilligar made a pair of wings out of silk and jumped off the roof of her barn, thinking she would be swept up to heaven. She died.

The Millerite movement later evolved into the Seventh-day Adventist Church, which today boasts seven million members worldwide. A bastion of apocalyptic theology, the church teaches that as Armageddon approaches, wickedness will increase and the Antichrist will preside over a global military and economic dictatorship. It is not all that surprising that their doctrines echo those of David Koresh: the Branch Davidians are an Adventist offshoot.

In the past three decades in Canada, Adventists and other apocalyptic preachers have found Quebec a particularly fertile recruiting ground. Some observers claim that such movements fill a vacuum created by Quebec's Quiet Revolution, which forced the Roman Catholic Church into retreat. Others say the phenomenon is intertwined with a sense of alienation stemming from Quebec's rapid industrialization.

Whatever the explanation, there is no question that Luc Jouret was only following in the footsteps of others before him. One of those figures was Roch Thériault, a bankrupt wood carver from Thetford Mines, Que., who was a recruiter for the Seventh-day Adventists before breaking away to form his own cult. Like Jouret's Order of the Solar Temple, Thériault's sect supported itself with a bakery and holistic healing services. The bearded cult leader convinced his disciples to establish a commune in the wilderness by claiming that he was an emissary of God, that they were the chosen people and that the world would end on Feb. 17, 1979. What did happen was that Thériault took eight of his female followers as wives, and spent the next decade committing horrible atrocities, including amputations and castrations. . . .

While many dismiss the apocalyptic prophecies of the Thériaults and Jourets as the ravings of a lunatic fringe, those beliefs have much in common with the core of mainstream religion. Practically every Christian church embraces the concepts of the Second Coming and Judgment Day. In a 1983 Gallup poll, 62 per cent of Americans expressed "no doubt" that Christ would return to Earth some time in the future. And in an Angus Reid poll of Canadians in 1993, fully 30 per cent of respondents said that would happen in the next 100 years. There is nothing alien about such views: they belong to a 2,000-year-old Western tradition.

CULTS AND THE APPROACH OF THE MILLENNIUM

Richard Lacayo

Many individuals and groups expect the year 2000 to usher in great changes in society and the world. Richard Lacayo, a senior writer for *Time*, reports that "millennial fever" has inspired the formation of new, bizarre, and sometimes dangerous cults that have created their own doctrines to interpret the meaning of the coming millennium. Some of these groups have advocated suicide as a means of reaching a higher plane of consciousness, he notes. Other recent events have also fostered the spread of cults, the author contends; in particular, the stellar rise of the Internet has enabled users to easily explore a wide array of belief systems. Because the Internet is so far-reaching, asserts Lacayo, it provides cults with a powerful tool with which to recruit members from around the world.

On Saturday, March 22, 1997, around the time that the disciples of Heaven's Gate were just beginning their quiet and meticulous self-extinction [in Rancho Santa Fe, California], a small cottage in the French Canadian village of St.-Casimir exploded into flames. Inside the burning house were five people, all disciples of the Order of the Solar Temple. Since 1994, 74 members of that group have gone to their death in Canada, Switzerland and France. In St.-Casimir the dead were Didier Quèze, 39, a baker, his wife Chantale Goupillot, 41, her mother and two others of the faithful. At the last minute the Quèze children, teenagers named Tom, Fanie and Julien, opted out. After taking sedatives offered by the adults, they closeted themselves in a garden shed to await their parents' death. Police later found them, stunned but alive.

For two days and nights before the blast, the grownups had pursued a remarkable will to die. Over and over they fiddled with three tanks of propane that were hooked to an electric burner and a timing device. As many as four times, they swallowed sedatives, then arranged themselves in a cross around a queen-size bed, only to rise in bleary frustration when the detonator fizzled. Finally, they blew themselves to kingdom come. For them that would be the star Sirius, in the constellation Canis Major, nine light-years from Quebec. According to the doctrines of the Solar Temple, they will reign there forever, weightless and serene.

Quite a mess. But no longer perhaps a complete surprise. Eighteen years after [the mass suicide of Jim Jones' followers at] Jonestown, suicide cults have entered the category of horrors that no longer qualify as shocks. Like plane crashes and terrorist attacks, they course roughly for a while along the nervous system, then settle into that part of the brain reserved for bad but familiar news. As the bodies are tagged and the families contacted, we know what the experts will say before they say it. That in times of upheaval and uncertainty, people seek out leaders with power and charisma. That the established churches are too fainthearted to satisfy the wilder kinds of spiritual hunger. That the self-denial and regimentation of cult life will soften up anyone for the kill.

The body count at Rancho Santa Fe is a reminder that this conventional wisdom falls short. These are the waning years of the 20th century, and out on the margins of spiritual life there's a strange phosphorescence. As predicted, the approach of the year 2000 is coaxing all the crazies out of the woodwork. They bring with them a twitchy hybrid of spirituality and pop obsession. Part Christian, part Asian mystic, part Gnostic, part *X-Files*, it mixes immemorial longings with the latest in trivial sentiments. When it all dissolves in overheated computer chat and harmless New Age vaporings, who cares? But sometimes it matters, for both the faithful and the people who care about them. Sometimes it makes death a consummation devoutly, all too devoutly, to be desired.

So the worst legacy of Heaven's Gate may yet be this: that 39 people sacrificed themselves to the new millennial kitsch. That's the cultural by-product in which spiritual yearnings are captured in New Age gibberish, then edged with the glamour of sci-fi and the consolations of a toddler's bedtime. In the Heaven's Gate cosmology, where talk about the end of the world alternates with tips for shrugging off your fleshly container, the cosmic and the lethal, the enraptured and the childish come together. Is it any surprise then that it led to an infantile apocalypse, one part applesauce, one part phenobarbital? Look at the Heaven's Gate Website. Even as it warns about the end of the world, you find a drawing of a space creature imagined through insipid pop dust-jacket conventions: aerodynamic cranium, big doe eyes, beatific smile. We have seen the Beast of the Apocalypse. It's Bambi in a tunic.

By now, psychologists have arrived at a wonderfully elastic profile of the people who attach themselves to these intellectual chain gangs: just about anybody. Applicants require only an unsatisfied spiritual longing, a condition apt to strike anyone at some point in life. Social status is no indicator of susceptibility and no defense against it. For instance, while many of the dead at Jonestown were poor, the Solar Temple favors the carriage trade. Its disciples have included the wife and son of the founder of the Vuarnet sunglass company. The Branch Davidians at Waco came from many walks of life. And at Rancho Santa Fe they were paragons of the entrepreneurial class, so well organized they died in shifts.

Proliferation of Cults

The U.S. was founded by religious dissenters. It remains to this day a nation where faith of whatever kind is a force to be reckoned with. But a free proliferation of raptures is upon us, with doctrines that mix the sacred and the tacky. The approach of the year 2000 has swelled the ranks of the fearful and credulous. On the Internet, cults multiply in service to Ashtar and Sananda, deities with names you could find at a perfume counter, or to extraterrestrials—the Zeta Reticuli, the Draconian Reptoids—who sound like softball teams at the Star Wars cantina. Carl Raschke, a cult specialist at the University of Denver, predicts "an explosion of bizarre and dangerous" cults. "Millennial fever will be on a lot of minds."

As so often in religious thinking, the sky figures importantly in the New Apocalypse. For centuries the stars have been where the meditations of religion, science and the occult all converged. Now enter Comet Hale-Bopp. In an otherwise orderly and predictable cosmos, where the movement of stars was charted confidently by Egyptians and Druids, the appearance of a comet, an astronomical oddity, has long been an opportunity for panic. When Halley's comet returned in 1910, an Oklahoma religious sect, the Select Followers, had to be stopped by the police from sacrificing a virgin. In the case of Hale-Bopp, for months the theory that it might be a shield for an approaching UFO has roiled the excitable on talk radio and in Internet chat rooms like—what else?—*alt.conspiracy.*

Astronomical charts may also have helped determine the timing of the Heaven's Gate suicides. They apparently began on the weekend of March 22–23, 1997, around the time that Hale-Bopp got ready to make its closest approach to Earth. That weekend also witnessed a full moon and, in parts of the U.S., a lunar eclipse. For good measure it included Palm Sunday, the beginning of the Christian Holy Week. Shrouds placed on the corpses were purple, the color of Passiontide, or, for New Agers, the color of those who have passed to a higher plane.

The Heaven's Gate philosophy added its astronomical trappings to a core of weirdly adulterated Christianity. Then came a whiff of Gnosticism, the old heresy that regarded the body as a burden from which the fretful soul longs to be freed. From the time of St. Paul, some elements of Christianity have indulged an impulse to subjugate the body. But like Judaism and Islam, it ultimately teaches reverence for life and rejects suicide as a shortcut to heaven.

The modern era of cultism dates to the 1970s, when the free inquiry of the previous decade led quite a few exhausted seekers into intellectual surrender. Out from the rubble of the countercultures came such groups as the Children of God and the Divine Light Mission, est and the Church of Scientology, the robotic political followers of Lyndon LaRouche and the Unification Church of the Rev. Sun Myung Moon. On Nov. 18, 1978, the cultism of the '70s arrived at its dark crescendo in Jonestown, Guyana, where more than 900 members of Jim Jones' Peoples Temple died at his order, most by suicide.

Since then two developments have fostered the spread of cultism. One is the end of communism. Whatever the disasters of Marxism, at least it provided an outlet for utopian longings. Now that universalist impulses have one less way to expend themselves, religious enthusiasms of whatever character take on a fresh appeal. And even Russia, with a rich tradition of fevered spirituality and the new upheavals of capitalism, is dealing with modern cults.

Imported sects like the Unification Church have seen an opening there. Homegrown groups have also sprung up. One surrounds a would-be messiah named Vissarion. With his flowing dark hair, wispy beard and a sing-song voice full of aphorisms, he has managed to attract about 5,000 followers to his City of the Sun. Naturally it's in Siberia, near the isolated town of Minusinsk. According to reports in the Russian press, Vissarion is a former traffic cop who was fired for drinking. In his public appearances, he speaks of "the coming end" and instructs believers that suicide is not a sin. Russian authorities are worried that he may urge his followers on a final binge. In the former Soviet lands, law enforcement has handled cults in the old Russian way, with truncheons and bars. Some have been banned. In 1996 a court in Kiev gave prison terms to leaders of the White Brotherhood, including its would-be messiah, Marina Tsvigun.

The second recent development in cultism is strictly free market and technological. For the quick recruitment of new congregations, the Internet is a magical opportunity. It's persuasive, far reaching and clandestine. And for better and worse, it frees the imagination from the everyday world. "I think that the online context can remove people from a proper understanding of reality and of the proper tests for truth," says Douglas Groothuis, a theologian and author of *The Soul in Cyberspace*. "How do you verify peoples' identity? How do you connect 'online' with real life?"

"The Internet allows different belief systems to meet and mate," adds Stephen O'Leary, author of *Arguing the Apocalypse*, which examines end-of-the-world religions. "What you get is this millennial stew, a mixture of many different belief systems." Which is the very way that the latest kinds of cultism have flourished. As it happens, that's also the way free thought develops generally. Real ideas sometimes rise from the muck, which is why free societies willingly put up with so much muck.

In Gustave Flaubert's story *A Simple Heart*, an old French woman pines for a beloved nephew, a sailor who has disappeared in Cuba. Later she acquires a parrot. Because it comes from the Americas, it reminds her of him. When the parrot dies, she has it stuffed and set in her room among her items of religious veneration. On her death-bed, she has a vision of heaven. The clouds part to reveal an enormous parrot.

The lessons there for Heaven's Gate? The religious impulse sometimes thrives on false sentiment, emotional need and cultural fluff. In its search for meaning, the mind is apt to go down some wrong paths and to mistake its own reflection for the face of God. Much of the time, those errors are nothing more than episodes of the human comedy. Occasionally they become something worse. This is what happened at Rancho Santa Fe, where foolish notions hardened into fatal certainties. In the arrival of Comet Hale-Bopp, the cult members saw a signal that their lives would end soon. There are many things about which they were badly mistaken. But on that one intuition, they made sure they were tragically correct.

CULTS AND THE NEW AGE MOVEMENT

Erica Goode

In the following selection, Erica Goode writes that many members of modern society have become disenchanted with traditional religions, propelling religious experimentation in new directions. In this atmosphere, argues Goode, the cultish New Age movement has flourished. A mixture of science fiction, witchcraft, and unconventional religious practices, the New Age movement offers individuals a wide variety of spiritual beliefs which they can tailor to their own needs or preferences, Goode observes. Some of these practices and beliefs may seem outlandish or misguided, she asserts, yet the New Age movement can provide needy followers with an alternative to organized religion and a tantalizing pathway to spiritual enlightenment. However, when New Age spirituality is combined with a mesmerizing and powerful cult leader, Goode warns, the results can be disastrous, as evidenced by the mass suicide of members of the Heaven's Gate cult in 1997.

Left behind were telling images: a suitcase packed by the bedside, a "Red Alert" message flashing on a World Wide Web page, silent computer workstations in a starkly furnished mansion, a picture of an extraterrestrial that—disappointingly—looked like every other depiction of alien beings.

If [Heaven's Gate leader] Marshall Applewhite was deluded about the finer points of astronomy, mistaken about the urgency of his situation, unimaginative in his conception of alien life-forms, he was right about one thing. Events, in their unfolding, carry messages. They can be mined for meaning. The mass suicide of a religious cult is no exception.

Fanaticism is a measure not so much of content as of degree. And while the followers of Applewhite, also known as "Do," chose an unusual—most would say crackpot—means of ascent, the farewell message sent by a woman before her death at Rancho Santa Fe, California, had a certain universal ring. "They had a formula of how to get out of the human kingdom to a level above humans," she said. "And I said to myself, 'That's what I want. That's what I've been looking for.'. . . I've been on this planet for 31 years, and there's nothing here for me."

Subtract the spaceship and the mass suicide, and you have a yearning and a search familiar to millions of Americans—one that has found a home in the New Age movement, a collection of religious practices, therapy techniques, witchcraft, science fiction, and alternative medicine.

The believers are in the condo next door, the office down the hall. An insurance company administrator, a woman in her mid-40s with two children, believes that one night in the late 1970s, on a country road in southeastern Michigan, she witnessed the landing of a UFO. A 29-year-old law student, working at a public prosecutor's office in Pennsylvania, believes the Native American medicine bag he wears around his neck will keep him safe and "always lead me back home." A 57-year-old business consultant keeps crystals in his house.

According to the American Booksellers Association, the sale of New Age books jumped from 5.6 million copies in 1992 to 9.7 million in 1995. Close to $2 billion, according to *Forbes* magazine, is spent each year in the United States on aromatherapists, channelers, macrobiotic food vendors, and other aids to spiritual and physical well-being. And in a 1994 Roper poll, 45 percent of those who responded agreed that meditation had given them "a strong sense of being in the presence of something sacred."

Coming of Age

Indeed, if the extremes of a society are a kind of fun-house mirror—a distortion and exaggeration of normal life—then Rancho Santa Fe can be seen as proof that New Age has come of age, an influence robust enough to make its mark in tragedy. Just as the 1995 Oklahoma City bombing [of a federal building] displays the extreme of Americans' distrust of government, the mass suicide of Applewhite's comet-struck followers is a grotesque extension of a now well-established parallel universe of alternative theology, and a widespread fascination with paranormal phenomena, self-exploration, and spirituality in general. The members of Heaven's Gate were in tune with their time. They designed Web sites. They got their cars washed. They wore Nikes.

The line between religion and cult, between faith and zealotry, is often difficult to draw. Many religions—Jehovah's Witnesses and Seventh-Day Adventists, for example—were once considered cults. And in the United States, there are as many as 3,500 "new" religious groups, many with beliefs as seemingly outlandish as that of Applewhite and his followers. The millennium, disenchantment with organized religion, and the isolation of late 20th-century life have steered religious experimentation in new directions. The New Age offers a menu of spiritual choices. "What a lot of people will do," says a San Francisco man who combines Hindu mysticism and Tibetan Buddhism in his religious life, "is to take a little from each [New Age theme] and combine them. . . . It's like making soup."

He is standing in Fields Book Store on Polk Street, one of the oldest metaphysical bookstores. Fields carries titles that range from classics like Thoreau's *Walden* to tomes on Eastern meditation techniques, to bestsellers like *The Celestine Prophecy.* On the periodical shelf are New Age magazines including *Common Boundary, Gnosis,* and *New Worlds.*

New Age Railroad

Gateways bookstore in Santa Cruz, 80 miles south of San Francisco, markets harmonic wind chimes, videos, and New Age music as well as books. Its bulletin board advertises seminars in aromatherapy, mountain walking meditation, and harmonic synchronistic attunement. Santa Cruz is a popular stop on the New Age railroad, whose tracks also run through Eugene, Ore.; Boulder, Colo.; Santa Fe, N.M.; Sedona, Ariz.; Madison, Wis., and other spiritual meccas. A devoted seeker could spend the better part of a lifetime—and an enormous amount of money—roving from town to town, learning to channel spirits, revisit past lives, or share stories of alien abductions.

Astrological events are often seen as having significance for human destiny, as are important dates in the New Testament. Excitement over the "Harmonic Convergence" in 1987 brought New Age thinking into the media spotlight. The conjunction of Neptune and Uranus in the early 1990s was considered by many to augur the end of one existence and the beginning of another. "After all," says Richard Smoley, editor of *Gnosis,* "the whole idea of the New Age is that some kind of new age is going to dawn."

To Smoley, the addition of UFOs and extraterrestrials to the New Age soup is easy to explain: They are the postmodern equivalents of ghosts, angels, fairies, elves—the 20th-century rebuilding of pagan pantheons. "People have always seen the earth as inhabited by conscious beings other than ourselves," he says. "Today, the mythic sensibility has been affected enough by science that people see those other intelligences as extraterrestrial." Books chronicling UFO encounters—*Project Earth* by Ida Kanneberg and *The Alien Abduction Survival Guide* by Michelle LaVigne are two examples—have a wide audience. Psychologist Carl Jung, writing about flying saucers in 1958, saw belief in such phenomena as a projection of a higher self to which humans aspire.

If "faith" is the root of mainstream Christianity, "communication" is the stamen of many New Age flowerings. "For the more futuristic New Agers, the self is conceived as an information-processing entity which changes nature depending on the information flows it receives and the various media to which it connects," writes Erik Davis in the *Southern*

Atlantic Quarterly. Because of this emphasis on communication, Davis says, "channeling" plays a crucial role. It is the 20th-century equivalent of the Oracle at Delphi, of "19th-century table-rapping," an "immediate but controlled" mode of nonrational communication. The Internet also fits nicely into New Age practice. It offers unrivaled opportunities to spread the word, and the Net surfer can send his spirit around the world, literally "shedding his container."

To Know Thyself

Yet what New Age cultivars have in common with each other may be best summarized by the name of Smoley's magazine, *Gnosis*, the ancient Greek word for knowledge. Ancient Gnosticism coexisted with and influenced Christianity in the first and second centuries A.D., but was smothered as heretical soon after. Its central tenet, outlined in second-century texts that were rediscovered in 1945, is that self-knowledge is knowledge of God: The self and God are one and the same. This precept links Gnosticism—and its many derivatives— more closely with Eastern metaphysical systems and paganism than with mainstream Christianity.

For a generation of lapsed Catholics, Protestants and Jews, the do-it-yourself aspect of self-knowledge is an attractive alternative to organized religion. The pursuit of enlightenment needs no intermediaries, no tedious Sunday sermons, no church socials or collection plates. There is no hierarchy, no central religious figure. In Gnostic terms, Christ was an illuminated teacher who brought the world gnosis, rather than the son of God who died to atone for human sins.

Yet fealty to a powerful, charismatic leader is the antithesis of Gnosticism and its New Age offshoots. And what creates a Jonestown or a Rancho Santa Fe is exactly that. Applewhite, and others like him, exploit universal needs: the craving to belong, the desire for orderliness and certainty, the wish to connect to something larger than oneself, the secret hope of finding an all-caring parent who offers protection and comfort.

Most cult members are ordinary people who, during a moment of vulnerability, meet someone who introduces them to a new way of thinking. "Nobody wakes up one morning and says, 'I think I should join a group that says that when a comet comes, we should all kiss ourselves good-bye,'" says Clark McCauley, a Bryn Mawr College psychology professor. Rather, the reality of the outside world dissolves gradually, eroded by seduction and authority. The new recruit may hardly notice the slow shifting of his world view.

Demands of the Cult

Isolation, a specialty of brainwashers of all kinds, is the most potent weapon wielded by a Marshall Applewhite or a Jim Jones. David Geoffrey Moore, who died in the mansion at Rancho Santa Fe, told his mother, for example, that having contact with his family would hinder the group's goals and "tug at their vibrational level." For the most part, the members of a cult submit gladly to the increasing demands put on them by the leader, much as a churchgoer may happily participate in fund-raising drives, bake sales, or auctions. The cult's demands for time, money, and sacrifice are seen as ways to prove commitment to the cause. But while the members of a traditional congregation can decline to participate, and return after the service to their families and jobs, cult members have too much to lose if they refuse. "People affiliate with religions, but people become addicted to cults," says Benjamin Zablocki, a Rutgers University sociologist.

In the hands of a leader whose thinking has become paranoid and bizarre, such dependence can be fatal. "You can follow us, but you cannot stay here and follow us," Do told his followers in the videotape made just before they died. In the antiseptic, sexless world of perfect order he had created, a world of barren white walls and metal bunk beds, devoid of human clutter, they believed him.

Cults and UFO Mythology

Paul Kurtz

Paul Kurtz is the founder and chairman of the Committee for the Scientific Investigation of Claims of the Paranormal (CSICOP), an organization that promotes empirical scientific inquiry of paranormal claims. In the following article, Kurtz analyzes the doctrine of Heaven's Gate followers, who committed collective suicide in 1997 so that they could, according to their beliefs, ascend to a higher plane of existence via a UFO spacecraft. Their paranormal theology, in Kurtz's view, is partly the result of an inability to think critically and scientifically—an inability shared by large sectors of the public. He places a substantial amount of the blame for this phenomenon on the mass media, arguing that the media have irresponsibly presented fantastical tales of the paranormal as being based in fact. The result, concludes Kurtz, is the proliferation of "cults of unreason," or groups that are not able to distinguish between reality and science fiction.

Heaven's Gate has stunned the world. Why would thirty-nine seemingly gentle and earnest people in Rancho Santa Fe, California, voluntarily commit collective suicide? They left us eerie messages on videotapes, conveying their motives: they wished to leave their "containers" (physical bodies) in order to ascend to a new plane of existence, a Level Above Human.

It was a celestial omen, Comet Hale-Bopp, that provoked their departure. For they thought that it carried with it a UFO spacecraft—an event already proclaimed on the nationally syndicated Art Bell radio show when Whitley Strieber and Courtney Brown maintained that a spaceship "extraterrestrial in origin" and under "intelligent control" was tracking the comet. According to astronomer Alan Hale, co-discoverer of the comet, what they probably saw was a star behind the comet. Interestingly, the twenty-one women and eighteen men, ranging in ages from twenty-one to seventy-two, seemed like a cross section of American citizens—though they demonstrated some degree of technical and engineering skills, and some even described themselves as "computer nerds." They sought to convey their bizarre UFO theology

Reprinted from Paul Kurtz, "UFO Mythology: The Escape to Oblivion," *Skeptical Inquirer*, July/August 1997, by permission of *Skeptical Inquirer*.

on the Internet. Were these people crazy, a fringe group, overcome by paranoia? Or were there other, deeper causes at work in their behavior?

Heaven's Gate was led by Marshall Herff Applewhite and Bonnie Lu Nettles (who died in 1985), who taught their followers how to enter the Kingdom of God. They believed that some 2,000 years ago beings from an Evolutionary Level Above Human sent Jesus to teach people how to reach the true Kingdom of God. But these efforts failed. According to documents left on the Heaven's Gate Web site, "In the early 1970s, two members of the Kingdom of Heaven (or what some might call two aliens from space) incarnated into two unsuspecting humans in Houston [Applewhite and Nettles]. . . ." Over the next twenty-five years Applewhite and Nettles transmitted their message to hundreds of followers. Those who killed themselves at Rancho Sante Fe (including Applewhite)—plus the two former members who subsequently attempted to take their lives on May 6, 1997, one of them succeeding—did so to achieve a higher level of existence.

A Cult of Unreason

Reading about the strange behavior of this cult of unreason, one is struck by the unquestioning obedience that Applewhite was able to elicit from his faithful flock. There was a rigid authoritarian code of behavior imposed upon everyone, a form of mind control. Strict rules and rituals governed all aspects of their monastic lives. They were to give up all their worldly possessions, their diets were regulated, and sex was strictly forbidden (seven members, including Applewhite, were castrated). The entire effort focused on squelching the personal self. Independent thinking was discouraged.

The followers of Heaven's Gate lived under a siege morality; they were super-secretive, attempting to hide their personal identities. They were like nomads wandering in the wilderness, seeking the truths of a Higher Revelation from extraterrestrial semi-divine beings. What has puzzled so many commentators is the depth of their conviction that space aliens were sending envoys to Earth and abducting humans. They kept vigils at night, peering for streaks of light that might be UFOs, waiting for spacecraft to arrive.

We read on their Web page: "We suspect that many of us arrived in staged spacecraft (UFO) crashes, and many of our discarded bodies (genderless, not belonging to the human species), were retrieved by human authorities (government and military)."

The Media and Pseudoscience

This form of irrational behavior should be no surprise to the readers of the *Skeptical Inquirer*. I submit that the mass media deserve a large share of the blame for this UFO mythology. Book publishers and TV and movie producers have fed the public a steady diet of science fiction fantasy packaged and sold as real. Alarmed by the steady stream of irresponsible programming spewing forth claims that were patently false, in 1996 CSICOP (the Committee for the Scientific Investigation of Claims of the Paranormal), publisher of *Skeptical Inquirer*, established the Council for Media Integrity, calling for some balanced presentation of science. We said that, given massive media misinformation, it is difficult for large sectors of the public to distinguish between science and pseudoscience, particularly since there is a heavy dose of "quasi-documentary" films. Why worry about these programs? Because, I reply, the public, with few exceptions, does not have careful, critical knowledge of paranormal and pseudoscientific claims. So far, the Council for Media Integrity's warnings have gone largely unheeded. What drivel NBC, Fox, and other networks have produced! (A notable exception to this is ABC, which we are glad to say has called upon CSICOP skeptics to present alternative views on *20/20*, *Prime Time*, and other shows.) TV is a powerful medium; and when it enters the home with high drama and the stamp of authenticity, it is difficult for ordinary persons to distinguish purely imaginative fantasies from reality. Many people blame the Internet. I think the media conglomerates, who sell their ideas as products, are to blame, not the Internet. We are surely not calling for censorship, only that some measure of responsibility be exercised by editors and producers. Interestingly, the Heaven's Gaters were avid watchers of TV paranormal programs.

CSICOP and the *Skeptical Inquirer* have been dealing with UFO claims on a scientific basis for more than twenty years. We have attempted to provide, wherever we could, scientific evaluations of the claims. We have never denied that it is possible, indeed probable, that other forms of life, even intelligent life, exist in the universe. And we support any effort to verify such an exciting hypothesis. But this is different from the belief that we are now being visited by extraterrestrial beings in spacecraft, that they are abducting people, and that there is a vast government coverup of these alien invasions—a "Luciferian" conspiracy, according to Heaven's Gate.

Space-Age Religion

In my view, what we are dealing with is "the transcendental temptation," the tendency of many human beings to leap beyond this world to other dimensions, impervious to the tests of evidence and the standards of logical coherence, the temptation to engage in magical thinking. UFO mythology is similar to the message of the classical religions where God sends his Angels as emissaries who offer salvation to those who accept the faith and obey his Prophets. Today, the chariots of the gods are UFOs. What we are witnessing in the past half century is the spawning of a New Age religion. (This year marks the fiftieth anniversary of Kenneth Arnold's sighting of the first flying saucers over the State of Washington in 1947.)

There are many other signs that UFO mythology has become a space-age religion and that it is not based on scientific evidence so much as emotional commitment. Witness the revival of astrology today; or the growth of Scientology, which proposes space-age reincarnation to their Thetans and attracts famous movie stars such as Tom Cruise and John Travolta; or the Order of the Solar Temple, in which seventy-four people committed suicide in Switzerland, Quebec, and France, waiting to be transported to the star Sirius, nine light-years away. Perhaps one of the most graphic illustrations of this phenomenon is what occurred on April 21, 1997, when the cremated remains of twenty-four people, including Gene Roddenberry (father of *Star Trek*), Timothy Leary (former Harvard guru), and Gerard O'Neill (scientific promoter of space colonies), were catapulted into space from the Grand Canary island off of the Moroccan coast aboard an American Pegasus rocket. This celestial burial is symptomatic of the New Age religion, in which our sacred church is outer space. The religious temptation enters when romantic expectations outreach empirical capacities.

Scientific Inquiry

Science is based on factual observation and verification. It was perhaps best illustrated by the discovery of Comet Hale-Bopp. That the comet has been captured by the paranormal imagination and transformed into a religious symbol is unfortunate. Alan Hale deplored this extrapolation of his observations. Yet the transcendental temptation can at times be so powerful that it knows no bounds.

Incidentally, the paranormal—which means, literally, that which is alongside of or beside normal scientific explanation—was involved in other aspects of the Heaven's Gate theology. The members expressed beliefs in astrology, tarot cards, psychic channeling, telepathy, resurrection, and reincarnation. That is why it is often difficult to ferret out and examine these claims dispassionately, for New Agers are dealing with faith, credulity, and a deep desire to believe, rather than with falsifiable facts; and they are resistant to any attempt to apply critical thinking to such spiritual questions.

Quotations from the Heaven's Gate videotape are instructive. Those who committed suicide affirmed that: "We are looking forward to this. We are happy and excited." "I think everyone in this class wants something more than this human world has to offer." "I just can't wait to get up there." These testimonials sound like those of born-again fundamentalists who are waiting for the Rapture and whose beliefs are self-validating. These confirmations of faith are not necessarily true; they are accepted because they have a profound impact on the believers' lives. Heaven's Gate gave meaning and purpose to the lives of its followers. As such, it performed an existential, psychological function similar to that of other religious belief systems. Obedience to a charismatic leader offered a kind of sociological unity similar to that provided by traditional belief systems.

Similarities to Established Religions

One might well ask, what is the difference between the myth of salvation of Heaven's Gate and many orthodox religious belief systems that likewise promise salvation to the countless millions who suppress their sexual passions, submit to ritual and dogma, and abandon their personal autonomy, all in quest of immortality? Their behavior is similar to the more than nine hundred Jewish Zealots who committed suicide at Masada in 73 C.E., or the early Christians who willingly died for the faith, or the young Muslim Palestinians today who strap explosives to their bodies and blow themselves to kingdom come in the hope of attaining heaven. I recently visited Cairo and the Great Pyramid of Gizeh, where a ship of the dead had been uncovered. The Pharaohs had equipped a vessel to take them to the underworld, hoping thereby to achieve immortality after death. This has been transformed into a UFO craft in modern-day lingo.

The bizarre apocalyptic theology of Heaven's Gate is interpreted by its critics as absurd and ridiculous; yet it was taken deadly serious by its devotees, and a significant part of the UFO scenario is now accepted by large sectors of the public.

In one sense the New Age paranormal religions are no more fanciful than the old-time religions. Considered cults in their own day, they were passed down from generation to generation, but perhaps they are no less queer than the new paranormal cults. No doubt many in our culture will not agree with my application of skepticism to traditional religion—CSICOP itself has avoided criticizing the classical systems of religious belief, since its focus is on empirical scientific inquiry, not faith.

I am struck by the fact that the Seventh-day Adventists, Jehovah's Witnesses, Mormons, and Chassidic Jews were considered radical fringe groups when first proclaimed; today they are part of the conventional religious landscape, and growing by leaps and bounds. Perhaps the major difference between the established religions and the new cults of unreason is that the former religions have deeper roots in human history.

The Aum Shinri Kyo cult in Japan, which in 1995 released poison gas into a crowded subway station, killing twelve people, was made up of highly educated young people, many with advanced degrees. Unable to apply their critical thinking outside of their specialties, they accepted the concocted promises of their guru. Thus an unbridled cult of unreason can attract otherwise rational people.

The Quest for Salvation

The one thing I have discovered in more than two decades of studying paranormal claims is that a system of beliefs does not have to be true in order to be believed, and that the validation of such intensely held beliefs is in the eyes of the believer. There are profound psychological and sociological motives at work here. The desire to escape the trials and tribulations of this life and the desire to transcend death are common features of the salvation myths of many religious creeds. And they appear with special power and eloquence in the case of the misguided acolytes of Heaven's Gate, who, fed by an irresponsible media that dramatizes UFO mythology as true, found solace in a New Age religion of salvation, a religion whose path led them to oblivion.

THE ANTICULT MOVEMENT

James D. Tabor and Eugene V. Gallagher

In the following selection, excerpted from their book *Why Waco? Cults and the Battle for Religious Freedom in America,* James D. Tabor and Eugene V. Gallagher argue that the anticult movement is overly eager in its condemnation of cults. Cults and other new religions, the authors maintain, can benefit society by raising fundamental questions about societal problems and by offering alternatives to mainstream beliefs and lifestyles. In addition, Tabor and Gallagher assert, the United States thrives on diversity and the exchange of ideas, but the anticult movement threatens to keep cults from contributing their opinions to the public dialogue. Attempts to silence cults, they warn, violate the constitutional right to religious freedom and can only weaken the fundamental values of American democracy.

Anticult activists see themselves as involved in a battle for the heart and soul of America. Ironically, the groups they oppose often see themselves in the same way though they are more likely to focus on a chosen few. . . . The anticultists ruefully observe a society in which beliefs are quickly abandoned in favor of a new or exotic message presented with sufficient guile and flair. In that view, whatever success "cults" achieve testifies to the inherent weaknesses of contemporary American society, rather than to the personal situations of those who are attracted to such groups. On that point as well, cultbusters and cult members agree. Cults strive to provoke us to an unsparing examination of both self and society; they anticipate that we will find both wanting; and they claim to offer remedies for our individual and social problems. Cults offer a vision of an alternative society and a plan for implementing it. The anticult activists see a nation in which the necessary social support for traditional values no longer exists, and they see new and unconventional religions capitalizing on that weakness. In this view, "cults" appear a symptom, not a cause, a lamentable indication of the deterioration of a valued way of life.

Many new and unconventional religious movements offer a similar diagnosis of life in America today. They see inattention to spiritual matters, moral laxity, a weakening of communal ties, a failure to uphold biblical standards, and any number of other problems, and they offer their own solutions. Their innovative remedies often derive from their perception that they enjoy the privilege of divine revelation; and they typically demand a strong and uncompromising response.

Under the surface of the anticult position there is a pervasive dissatisfaction with the prevailing ethos of contemporary American society, which has made the supposed proliferation of "cults" possible. The anticultists' vigorous defense of traditional religion, the nuclear family, personal autonomy, and other core values against the challenge of the "cults" allows them to locate the vexing problems of Americans and American society outside themselves in a dangerous and alien "other." Cults *are* alien in many ways. In some cases, they introduce foreign beliefs and practices into American society; but in others, such as the Branch Davidians, they give distinctively different interpretations to common religious elements such as the biblical book of Revelation. However, cultbusters see "cults" as alien whatever their place of origin because they manifest psychological instability, moral evil, religious error, or any combination of the three. By portraying "cults" as the "other," cultbusters absolve themselves of any complicity in the problems they discuss.

Since "cults" represent an invasive presence, rather than an acceptable variation from the norm, anyone who rejects the cultbusters' values by participating in a "cult" is asserted to have acted under external compulsion, rather than as a result of a careful, rational choice. Such a view contrasts markedly to the democratic ideal of our society as an arena for competing and conflicting ideas, thriving on debate, differences, and diversity. In such a society, persuasiveness is valued, and minority views are welcomed, often proving their enduring value to the majority. To admit that one may join a new or unconventional religious group for "good" reasons leaves one's own choices and decisions open to evaluation and criticism. The anticult polemicists fend off such critique by denying that anyone in his or her "right mind" would join a "cult." Moreover, because affiliation is itself evidence of aberrant behavior, cultbusters can easily dismiss the diagnoses of American society that such groups offer and the remedies that they propose. They act as if they have nothing to learn and much to fear from the intruder. Their general response to "cults" is exemplified by the unheeding responses that government officials made to David Koresh's religious pronouncements during the 1993 siege at Mount Carmel in Waco, Texas. When Koresh spoke *his* truth, they heard only "Bible babble." Where the Branch Davidians saw a religious community prepared for the end of the world, the authorities saw an armed compound full of "hostages."

The cultbusters' opposition to new and unconventional religious groups depends not only on an image of a passive self but also on an image of a broadly *uniform society* whose values and ethical codes are commonly agreed upon. They see an American consensus and claim to speak for it. In their view, the uniformity of social values guarantees the integrity of the family, harmonious interpersonal relations, and overall social stability. Despite their emphasis on common values, however, cultbusters see their society as extremely fragile and besieged from without. Cult members also see the problems and weaknesses in contemporary American society, but they do not see the remedy in espousing a vaguely defined uniform set of core values without any secure links to a specific social group. Instead, they locate the remedy in the creation of an *ideal society,* a select voluntary association founded on intense commitment to explicit religious values. Their vision is often exclusive; it offers a path toward perfection for those willing to pursue it. That exclusivity, however, allows them to sharpen their critique of American society. Cults typically offer a closed system of internally consistent doctrine, such as Koresh's biblical interpretation, that is passionately espoused by the members of the elect and contributes to their distinctive individual and social identities. The exclusivity, passion, and sheer differentness that mark cult life have the potential to create considerable friction between members of the group and those outside. The Mount Carmel community maintained a sometimes uneasy, often bemused, and generally comfortable peace with its neighbors over the course of its sixty-year history. The introduction of [federal officials] who had neither personal nor doctrinal familiarity with the Branch Davidians was a scenario that presaged conflict.

The Problem with the Cultbusters

Opposition to so-called cults enables many Americans to condemn much of what they find wrong in their society by attributing it to the influence of an alien "other." That strategy allows opponents to draw clear and sharp lines between right and wrong, good and evil, and legitimate and illegitimate religion. It is based from the outset, however, on an unexamined reaction that presumes that one's own position is self-evidently true and unassailable. In that sense it represents a flight from self-examination, a refusal to think hard about one's own values and commitments, and an authoritarian willingness to impose one's views on others. It is a form of intellectual, spiritual, and social isolationism that denies the possibility of learning anything new or valuable from those significantly different from oneself. When such an attitude is adopted in defense of the fundamental values of American society, as it is by the cultbusters, it is out of tune with the demands of a democratic society, particularly one that is rapidly becoming more diverse. It provides constricting and oppressive answers to serious questions about how Americans should deal with any minority groups, however they are defined. At the same time, it raises the issue of whether those whose beliefs or way of life is unconventional should receive the same protection of the law that other minority groups enjoy. In sum, the cultbusters' appeal to a supposed consensus of values expresses a nostalgia for a homogeneous society that never existed, which can have pernicious effects.

Government action against new or unorthodox religious groups, advocated by some anticult workers, bodes ill not only for such movements but also for everyone in our society. It arrogates to the state a power that all must oppose and depends on a very restricted reading of the constitutional guarantee of free exercise of religion. New and unconventional religions provide some of the most vivid examples of nay-saying in contemporary American society. To enlist the state in an effort to control or eradicate such groups is to deprive our common life of an invigorating diversity, as well as to sanction its immense power to enforce conformity. The anticult activists' claim to support the fundamental values of American democratic society is undermined by their willingness to suppress the exercise of religious freedom and, moreover, to engage the state in that campaign. If the purpose of the First Amendment is to protect religions from the state, rather than the state from religion, there is no constitutional basis for enlisting the power of the state in the campaign against so-called cults. That does not mean that the state is impotent to punish illegal acts done in the name of religion, but that the intervention must be carried out through normal legal channels. A wholesale government crusade against "destructive cults," such as that championed after Waco, is illegitimate and unconstitutional.

CHAPTER 4

CULTS AND TRADITIONAL RELIGIONS

THE DIFFERENCE BETWEEN CULTS AND RELIGIONS

Benjamin Wittes

Most traditional religions exhibit some of the features common-ly associated with cults. For example, cults frequently discourage followers from associating with family and friends, while many religious groups sponsor retreats that likewise isolate members. Yet these similarities are superficial, writes Benjamin Wittes, who argues that cults are not legitimate religions. According to Wittes, the major difference between a cult and a religion is the way in which cults actively employ deceptive and confusing lan-guage to control adherents' minds. Specifically, Wittes contends, cults confuse their members by defining religious terms in ambiguous and imprecise ways until the words become virtually meaningless. The result, he charges, is a reduction in cult follow-ers' critical thinking skills—and thereby in their ability to resist the cult's belief system. Wittes is a reporter for *Legal Times* in Washington, D.C.

"The only difference between a cult and a religion is a hundred years," said the editor of a prominent Washington weekly in turning down a proposal for an article on the Church of Scientology. The par-ticular editor in question is devoutly secular, so it's not too surprising that he would paint the issue with such a broad brush. What's far more surprising is the number of religious individuals and organiza-tions who are on record as agreeing with him, either equating reli-gions and cults or insisting on the blurriness of any line that might separate them.

It might seem perverse for honestly religious people to group their faiths with those of the sadists and megalomaniacs who run most cults, but a growing number are doing just that. A substantial sector of religious America, for example, sees the 1993 firefight in Waco, Texas, [between members of the Branch Davidians and U.S. federal agents] as an attack on radical religion and places the cutting edge of religious freedom in the defense of cults' free exercise rights.

Reprinted from Benjamin Wittes, "The Scent of a Cult," *First Things*, January 1995, by permission of *First Things*.

The Line Between Cults and Religions

According to the commonly accepted criteria for defining cults, the line between cults and religions is fuzzy indeed. The Cult Awareness Network (CAN), a Chicago-based clearinghouse of information on cults, identifies the following seven characteristics of "destructive cults": mind control, charismatic leadership, deception, exclusivity, alienation, exploitation, and totalitarian worldview. But as Thomas Taylor writes in *Christianity Today*, "Almost all Christian denominations have some aspects that would fit into the many vague definitions of cults." In fact, not only Christian denominations but all religions exhibit aspects that at least superficially resemble the defining features of cults. Do cults use controlled hunger to break down the resistance of members? So do Jews on Yom Kippur. Do cults isolate members for indoctrination sessions? Many religions sponsor retreats. Do cult members live together and eschew the outside world? So do monks. Do cults tap their adherents for money? So do televangelists and virtually all congregations. Do cults use mind control? Ah, but isn't it precisely the purpose of all religions to alter the way their adherents perceive the world? Brainwashing would be a more useful description of cults if someone could identify exactly what the word means.

The difference between a cult and a religion, of course, lies in extremity. Cults generally exhibit all seven of the CAN's criteria, while religions generally don't, and cults exhibit them with far greater vigor than religions do. Judaism, for example, demands of its practitioners an occasional day without food; most cults systematically malnourish their members. Still, without identifying an aspect of cults that is not also an aspect of established religious movements, these two classes of organization appear more similar than they really are. The confusion I have described induces a natural concern among religious organizations that a crackdown on cults could presage a crackdown on mainstream religions. As Taylor warns, "'We,' who sometimes wish that the government would restrict the behavior of [cults], may someday become 'them,' the prospective subjects of scrutiny and regulation."

CAN's definition of cults, then, lacks what we might call a red flag—one additional, readily visible criterion that stands beyond such argumentation. I shall propose one—though not, be it understood, in order to define cults as beyond First Amendment protection. The slippery slope that Taylor fears is very real; and the interests of a free society generally—and religious people specifically—are probably best served by toleration of the broadest range of religious beliefs, no matter how vulgar. I offer this refinement, rather, in the interests of intellectual clarity and so that religious organizations don't confuse their constitutional defense of cults with some broader sense of commonality with them. Where this issue concerns the Supreme Court, in other words, it may be useful that a cult should be deemed a religion; nevertheless, it is necessary for us to understand why most Americans, properly, intuit a difference between the Scientologists and the Moonies on the one hand and the Lubavichers on the other.

Doublethink

The quickest way to detect a cult is to sniff for doublethink. The cult seeks control over its membership not by providing a coherent theological system but by providing the opposite: an unstable theology infinitely malleable to the needs of the cult's top echelon and uninterpretable at all times to anyone below that level. Specifically, the cult destabilizes its theology by controlling its religious language—through ambiguity, definitional reversals, and deliberate imprecision. What ultimately separates religions from cults is not that cults seek to control the minds of adherents but that they employ Orwellian doublethink to do so and use the cover of language to effect the far more outrageous means of control set forth by CAN.

The Unification Church's use of the word "Messiah" provides a case in point. Reverend Moon on several occasions has called himself the Messiah, and the Moonie sacred text, *Divine Principle*, declares flatly that the Messiah was born in Korea between the two world wars (Moon was born in 1920). At other times, however, the church hierarchy demurs on the question of Moon's divinity. More important, it's not entirely clear what the word Messiah means in the church's vocabulary—the word means different things at different times. Jesus was the Messiah, according to the Moonies, but he failed in his mission to unite the world under a single theocracy, because he didn't marry and have children. Moon, then, represents the Second Coming, though not the Second Coming as described in Revelation. The National Council of Churches (NCC), in a critique of Unification theology, questioned the "meaning and intelligibility" of the Moonie view of the Messiah. While the NCC's first concern was that the teachings were un-Christian, for our purposes the more important critique is their incoherence.

The comparison with Lubavich Hasidism [a Hasidic sect founded by Schneour Zalman in the eighteenth century] is instructive. Many (though by no means all) Lubavicher Hasidim believed that Menachem Mendel Schneerson was the Messiah. In sharp contrast with the Moonies, however, "Messiah" has the same specific meaning to Lubavichers as it does to all religious Jews. Two thousand years of post–Second Temple Judaism has provided a framework of Jewish messianism, and Lubavichers could define precisely and briefly what they meant when they called Schneerson "King Moshiach." By contrast, when reporter Colin McEnroe asked Unification Church spokesman Peter Ross whether Rev. Moon was the Messiah, Ross suggested in effect that the question was unanswerable. "Do you have two days?" he said to McEnroe. When the reporter asked whether Ross could give a summary explanation, Ross told him, "That is the short version."

The Moonies have likewise rendered meaningless a series of words connected to family. The church refers to itself as "the family," and members call each other "brother" and "sister." Moon calls himself and his wife the "true parents." At the same time, the church urges new recruits to cut off contact with their biological families (parents in particular). The purpose, of course, is to appropriate to the church those words people intuitively associate with loyalty, love, and obedience, and to disconnect those words from biological relationships. Yet even as Moon interrupts normal family relations and appropriates the authority of parents, church literature refers to family values, clearly referring not to the church family but to the traditional nuclear family.

Control over Language

The principal vehicle for imposing doublethink is control over language, a dramatic example here being the Church of Scientology, a pseudo-religious cult oriented around the writings of L. Ron Hubbard. Hubbard created a dialect that rivals George Orwell's Newspeak in its complexity and capacity for indoctrination. As journalist Stewart Lamont writes in *Religion Inc: The Church of Scientology*, "This org-speak is a feature of Scientology in which all terms are defined strictly and processes given technical names by Ron. Like the Red Queen, a word means what Ron says it means." Lamont further explains that this "org-speak is an alphabet soup of initials, jargon, and pseudo-technical expressions. This heightens the impression that a science is being taught and that it is esoteric and unavailable to the bungling ignoramuses in the outside world."

In Scientology courses, students are made to use a Hubbard-written dictionary to look up every unknown word in their texts. The dictionaries, according to Lamont, "define words the Hubbard way." In addition to the technical words, they include English words Hubbard wishes to redefine; he defines "having," for example, as "to be able to touch or permeate or to direct the disposition of." No other reference material is permitted to be used in reading Hubbard's texts. In other words, not only does the church control its source texts, it controls the tools with which the members process them. By its own definition, the Church *has* (directs the disposition of) the English language and thereby *has* its adherents' thoughts.

Political as well as religious cults can be distinguished from legitimate organizations by their use of doublethink. Though political cults espouse extremist ideologies, not extremist theologies, operationally they are virtually identical to religious cults, and they also go to great lengths to control the vocabularies of their members. Dennis King, in his book *Lyndon LaRouche and the New American Fascism*, describes how LaRouche turned his National Caucus of Labor Committees (NCLC) from a Trotskyite organization into an anti-Semitic neo-fascist group:

> LaRouche helped his followers overcome their moral qualms by reframing reality for them through semantic tricks and false syllogisms.
>
> The resulting belief system involved four layers: a redefinition of "Jew," a redefinition of "Nazi," a denial of the concept of "left" and "right" in politics (to totally disorient the believer); and, for Jewish LaRouchians, a guilt trip and special fears.

According to King, LaRouche distinguished between real and fake Jews, defining the latter as Zionists and practitioners of religious Judaism and calling them "Jews who are not Jews." Real Jews, according to LaRouche, are followers of Philo of Alexandria, a first-century Jewish thinker with no modern following other than the Jews of the LaRouche movement.

LaRouche's redefinition of "Nazi" is even more sinister. Writes King,

> He argued that Hitler was put into power by the Rothschilds and other wealthy Jews-who-are-not-really-Jews. These evil oligarchs invented Nazi racialism and brainwashed the Nazis to accept it. They then urged Hitler and his cronies to persecute the German Jews so the latter would flee to Palestine, where the Rothschilds had decided to set up a zombie state as a tool of their world domination. . . . Thus did LaRouche place the ultimate blame for Hitler's crimes on the Jews-who-are-not-Jews-but-really-are-the-Jews-anyway.

In LaRouche literature, the words "Nazi" and "Jew" are both used sometimes pejoratively and sometimes in praise. Moreover, Nazi beliefs and practices are pejoratively called Jewish, and Jewish political practices, both in the U.S. and in Israel, are pejoratively called Nazi.

On the other end of the political spectrum, the New Alliance Party (NAP) plays similar games. The left-wing cult is led by former LaRouche associate Dr. Fred Newman (although the titular leader is Dr. Lenora Fulani, who fronts for the party as its presidential candidate), who considers himself a modern Lenin and writes hardline Marxist political tracts. At the same time, the NAP is not above McCarthyite red-baiting towards its rivals on the left. The party's paper, the *National Alliance*, attacked former NAP member William Pleasant with the banner headline: "William Pleasant's Latest Writings: Communism's Stinking Corpse." In NAP language, the words "left," "Communist," and "Marxist-Leninist" are all positive when applied to the NAP itself, but they are also signals for a priori condemnation when referring to anyone else.

The Power of Cults

These semantic tricks are not simply oddities of a few isolated cults, but the very source of the cognitive power of cults, the means by which cults concentrate power at the top of the pyramid. Since mainstream religions don't control language, their religious authorities simply can't exercise the degree of power over membership that cult leaders can when they make an active effort to reduce the critical capacities of their adherents. Even religions that have historically concentrated extreme power in the hands of their leadership, the Mormons and the Lubavichers, for example, face a great deal more dissent within their ranks than the mildest of true cults. Without tampering with the definition of "Messiah," those Lubavich leaders who believe that Schneerson was the Messiah have not been able to make their view universally accepted within the movement. Now that the Rebbe is dead, it is an open question whether or not Schneerson's successors (whoever they turn out to be) will bring about such a redefinition. If they do—and the talk within the movement of Schneerson's imminent return might be the stirrings of that redefinition—Lubavich may yet evolve into a cult. In its current form, however, it has a long way to go.

The cult is no more a subset of religion than it is a subset of political party. While some cults orient themselves around ideology and some around theology (and some around self-discovery, and some around psychoanalysis), and they can thus appear to resemble religious or political organizations, cults actually constitute a phenomenon of their own. The free exercise clause [of the U.S. Constitution] protects any organization oriented around a theological worldview. It would be a grave error, however, to conclude that all who come under that protection have anything more in common than the protection itself.

CULTISH BELIEFS PARALLEL TRADITIONAL THEOLOGY

Ronald Steel

Hoping to ascend to heaven via a UFO spaceship, thirty-nine members of the Heaven's Gate cult committed collective suicide in March 1997. The event triggered intense coverage by the media, which typically portrayed the group's doctrine as odd or even lunatic. In contrast, Ronald Steel argues that the religious beliefs adhered to by members of Heaven's Gate were not particularly bizarre but rather had origins in traditional Christian theology. For example, he writes, many Christians profess a belief in a heavenly afterlife; the members of Heaven's Gate only differed in that they believed their vehicle to the holy sphere would be a spaceship. Steel concludes that every religion—even Christianity—seems strange to outsiders who do not accept the group's spiritual tenets. A historian and author, Steel is a contributing editor for the weekly periodical *New Republic*.

The most remarkable thing about the March 1997 ascension of thirty-nine souls to what they have described as the "Next Level" via a UFO is not the strangeness of their religious beliefs, but the extraordinary response that the event triggered. For days the media have been saturated with stories about the group, its leaders and adherents, its eschatology and the most minute details of its behavior and living arrangements. Newspapers have felt the need to take editorial positions on the issue—invariably bristling with self-righteous denunciation—while TV and radio repeat the story endlessly, like a mantra.

The media highlighted the story, figuring it would fascinate, and even touch, the public deeply. In that they were right, even though they rarely understood, or even tried to investigate, why. What they did do, interestingly, was seek to distance themselves as far as possible from the group's professed beliefs, as if they feared contamination. Even more, they assured the public that the group's religious beliefs were so bizarre that they must be considered lunatic. An editorial in *The New York Times*, for instance, proclaimed that it was the "rantings of a madman" that led his "wounded, foolish followers" to their demise. On "60

Reprinted from Ronald Steel, "Ordinary People," *The New Republic*, April 21, 1997, by permission of *The New Republic*. Copyright 1997, The New Republic, Inc.

Minutes," Lesley Stahl was openly disdainful as two former members of the group expressed sympathy for the teachings of their onetime leader.

Christian Roots

What is the reason for this deep hostility, matched by an equal, if not greater, fascination? It cannot be, despite assertions to the contrary, that there is something particularly unique or bizarre about the group's religious beliefs. These beliefs are, after all, firmly rooted in Christian theology, especially in early gnosticism.

The group's members believed that the soul was separate and superior to the body, that those who followed their spiritual leader and observed his teachings would be saved, and that they should transcend their attachment to money, sex and family life—all of which can be found in the teachings of Jesus Christ.

The media seemed particularly fascinated by the fact that some of the men voluntarily chose to be castrated in order to release themselves from the bondage of sexual desire. Stahl even triumphantly announced, as if taking personal credit for the event, that one of the former members of the group was soon to become a father. But one does not have to dig very deeply into Christian belief to find discussion of impurity and mortification of the flesh, let alone celibacy for Catholic priests. TV evangelists proclaim (but don't practice) the flesh-hatred of self-flagellating medieval monks. And the notion that the true believer will ascend to heaven, whether on the wings of angels or a spaceship (the modern equivalent), was no doubt something that the thirty-nine seekers learned as children in Sunday school.

Christianity teaches that sipping wine and nibbling a wafer is, in the proper circumstances, equivalent to drinking the blood and eating the flesh of Christ, that Jesus was born to a woman impregnated by the spirit of God rather than by the messy intercession of sexual congress, that he could cure lepers and feed vast multitudes with two fish and five loaves of bread, and that following his death he would ascend to heaven corporally as well as spiritually intact. Yet the beliefs of this religion, with its millions of adherents worldwide, are not routinely described in the media as "bizarre." Nor is Christianity described as a "cult." For what is a cult but a collection of believers, like the early Christians, who have not yet achieved dominant status?

This is not, be assured, to denigrate Christianity. Every religion is "bizarre" for those who do not accept its strictures or practice its tenets. Indeed, one could say that is the whole point of religions: they offer solace, explain mysteries, provide standards of behavior and offer the promise of escape to a better world. The Heaven's Gate group would appear to be particularly benign, and even praiseworthy, in that its members were gentle, industrious, supportive and kind to one another. They did not try to coerce others into joining them. All they asked was to be left alone.

But what about the mass suicide? Does this not indicate the group's "underlying pathology," as many in the press insisted? Not necessarily these days. Don't many Americans now believe that suicide is preferable to suffering from terminal illness? Nation-states and organized religions condemn suicide because it depletes their pool of adherents. But does this make it a "pathology"?

In its editorial denunciation of the group, the *Times* explained that, although mainstream faiths believe in "resurrection, the meaninglessness of the flesh, the primacy of the spirit, the conversion from the physical to the heavenly plane," they are superior because the "believer himself cannot choose the moment of ascension," only the "central deity" can. But in war, the true believer in most faiths has little compunction about deciding the moment of ascension for his infidel enemy. Does that put murder on a higher plane of morality than suicide? Those who engage in what theologians call "just wars" are blessed, while those who commit suicide are deemed to be damned or at least "pathological."

Separation from Society

While the media are not interested in these philosophical questions, they have, in their own inchoate [rudimentary] way, reflected the public's fascination with this ardent group of gentle souls who came together to seek fulfillment through belief, work and companionship. Neither violent nor lazy nor acquisitive, they practiced virtues that society preaches but prefers neither to observe nor reward. They separated themselves, insofar as they could, from both the intrusive state and the omnipresent culture of consumerism. They did not openly defy these powerful forces so much as seek to live removed from their demands.

In this they are not greatly different from another millennial group, the Shakers, who also professed celibacy, communal ownership, pacifism, separation from the world, equality of the sexes and freedom to leave the collective. This desire to achieve separation from a corrupt society, whether physically, as in the communes of Vermont and the enclaves of Montana, or spiritually, as in the multitude of religious sects that abound in ever greater numbers, is an undeniable force in American life. As the state and the mass culture become increasingly pervasive and demanding, so people, individually or in groups, are drawn to alternatives.

That is why this story has such resonance among Americans, and why the mass media's hostility is not reflected in the millions who see something of their own unfulfilled longings in these searchers. How striking it is that those who knew them—whether former group members or simply neighbors or employers—were not harsh in their judgments. Said one woman who had rented office space to them: "They were such happy people."

A RELIGIOUSLY BEREFT SOCIETY

David Gelernter

According to David Gelernter, the appeal of cults is directly related to the suppression of traditional religion in the public sphere of American life. Gelernter cites several examples, such as the Supreme Court's 1962 ban on prayer in public schools, as proof that the influence of traditional religion on American society has been greatly weakened. This environment of hostility toward traditional religion has led to the disintegration of religious meaning in society, he writes, opening the door for new beliefs and cults that flourish among individuals hungry for religion and spirituality. Sometimes, too, Gelernter contends, the consequences can be deadly, as when thirty-nine Heaven's Gate cult members committed suicide in Rancho Santa Fe, California, in 1997. Gelernter is a professor of computer science at Yale University.

Thirty-nine people killed themselves in Rancho Santa Fe, Calif., in March 1997. Did the Internet have something to do with it? The cultists ran a Web-page design business. They may have trolled for new members by sending E-mail to likely targets. They believed an alien spaceship was hiding behind the Hale-Bopp comet; they may have got the news over the Net, where rumors spread fast.

This alien spaceship, they decided, would pick them up, but only if they were dead. They took this in stride, and are reported to have been "very upbeat, very outgoing" on the videotape they left behind in lieu of a suicide note.

Blaming Technology

It is tempting to blame the Internet at least in part, but the Net is no more guilty than the rope industry is when people hang themselves. More likely, the tragedy stems from the fact that as a nation we have never been more confused about good and evil, righteousness and wickedness, God and man. Yet we would always rather blame technology than ourselves.

Some cult pulls in a cosmic signal portending apocalypse, and acts accordingly—it's a sad old story. Until March 1997, the mass suicides

Reprinted from David Gelernter, "A Religion of Special Effects," *The New York Times*, March 30, 1997, by permission. Copyright ©1997 by The New York Times.

of recent years—the People's Temple in Guyana, the Branch Davidians in Waco, the 74 members of the Order of the Solar Temple—were accomplished with no help from the Web. The Internet, we are told, is a terrifically potent spreader of rumors. Granted, but radio was more potent. (One memorable night in 1938, Orson Welles created widespread panic by broadcasting blow-by-blow reports of an invasion from Mars.)

If technology is to blame, why not blame the movies? It's clear that the cultists got their ideas about alien spaceships from Hollywood. But you can't really blame the movies. Technology merely highlights and underlines the text it is given. If you look at modern America and then at the Rancho Santa Fe suicides, you cannot help but conclude that this story is about religion, not technology.

Evidently, the cult's goal in recent years was to "overcome" any attachment to money, sex and family life, and to live in a strictly authoritarian community—a re-creation of the poverty, chastity and obedience of Christian holy orders. Its members seemed to reach repeatedly for traditional Christian ideas and come up bare—their souls needed religion but their minds were stocked only with Hollywood junk.

They wanted to talk about their condition as believers, but the term they came up with to describe themselves was "crew members." Life on earth was no good, they held, because it was dominated by "Luciferians" and "space aliens"—Christianity plus a vivid bit of science fiction. The theology tract at their Web site was called "An E.T. Presently Incarnate." This is Christian language—"et incarnatus est"—in the service of Hollywood special effects.

The Suppression of Traditional Religion

Granted, weird cults (including suicidal ones) have been around for a long time. What is new in today's America is that traditional religion has been suppressed for a generation. Not in the sense that believers are hounded into prison; "suppressed" in the sense that the public domain has been vigorously swept clean of it by judges and opinion leaders who are proud of what they are doing.

A few highlights: the Supreme Court outlawed prayer and Bible reading in the public schools (1962), forbade a public high school to display the Ten Commandments (1980), barred "moments of silence" in the classroom (1987), prohibited nonsectarian prayers at public school graduations (1992).

In a recent article in *The Public Interest*, Jeremy Rabkin described a 1995 case in which a Federal appeals court denied parents the right to sue their school system over a ninth-grade sex-education program produced by a company called Hot, Sexy and Safer Productions. The program called for children to blow up condoms and "share with each other" their facial expressions during orgasm. A society where Orgasm

Studies are protected in the public schools and the Ten Command-ments are forbidden isn't neutral on religion; it is actively against it.

Religious Disintegration

The old-line Protestant denominations are in deep trouble today, and Reform and Conservative Judaism are falling apart. Many of their leaders see their mission in social terms rather than God terms. This religious disintegration was symbolized in an article that ran in 1996 in *The New York Times*, headlined, "One Holiday That Retains Its Meaning." Thanksgiving, it was reported, is "the one day when the perennial love of togetherness and a festive meal still seems fresh."

Practicing Jews and Christians apparently shrugged off this curious report of the death of Christmas, Easter, Passover—the press has been known to get things wrong. Yet the article is almost certainly correct. Among the nation's elite, traditional religion is indeed dead and only Thanksgiving "retains its meaning."

The idea that suppressing religion in the public sphere could actually *mean* anything or have consequences is, for the average sophisti-cate, a proposition to snort at. Yet here we are as a nation starved for religion, and the hunger is fiercest at upper social levels, where people set up shop as Web-page designers. The fundamentalist churches are doing fine, but they don't do much business among the technological elite. When the old religions are reeling, people cobble together new ones. In spiritually ignorant times like ours the new ones won't be much good, generally speaking, but people need *something*.

Environmentalism is a favorite religion nowadays; its leaders are explicit about its spiritual side. You can't display the Ten Command-ments in public school these days, but teachers are encouraged to peddle recycling dogma. Environmentalism is not for everyone, though, and it seems likely that the tragedy of Heaven's Gate is the story of spiritually famished people whipping up a religion like island castaways piecing together, in their dire need, a semblance of civiliza-tion out of driftwood and spit.

So is the Supreme Court responsible for what happened in Rancho Santa Fe? Of course not. Nor is the American Civil Liberties Union. A person makes his own choices; there are plenty of practicing Jews and Christians today. But there is enough indirect guilt to go around.

For several decades in the middle of the twentieth century, the air in many American cities was filthy and made people sick. The smoke-belching factory downtown didn't kill the dying man in the suburbs; it merely added its bit to a mildly poisonous atmosphere that killed the weakest. Today's crusade against religion has done the same sort of thing. Most of us shrug it off. The crusaders keep hitting us, but we can take it. The stronger among us remain Christians and Jews in the old sense, or find satisfaction in America's new secular religions. The weaker join cults. The weakest die.

RELIGIOUS INTOLERANCE TOWARD CULTS

Stephen L. Carter

In the following excerpt from his book *The Culture of Disbelief: How American Law and Politics Trivialize Religious Devotion,* Stephen L. Carter argues that society's antipathy toward cults and religions that lie outside the mainstream is wrong. He writes that there will always be individuals and groups whose religious commitments may appear eccentric and even bizarre. Yet no one, Carter charges, is qualified to distinguish between a bona fide religion and a cult. Permitting a broad range of religious practices and beliefs to flourish is in the best interest of society, according to Carter, for toleration breeds religious freedom. Carter is a legal scholar who writes and lectures extensively on legal, political, and religious subjects.

One of [my children's] favorite films is that much-beloved family classic, *The Sound of Music.* They have watched the videotape so often that my wife and I sometimes wonder whether there is a single line of dialogue that they have not committed to memory. We are glad they like the film, because it tells a clear, clean, spiritually uplifting story, in which the protagonists rely on wits and faith for their survival, instead of the ruthless destruction of the opposition that is today a staple of "children's" programming. Because the kids so enjoy the story and the music, we decided one fine June weekend to take them to visit the Trapp Family Lodge, nestled in the rolling green hills above Waterbury, Vermont. There, we thought, the children might learn about the connection—or, perhaps, the disconnection—between art and life. So off we went on a grand family outing. The children got a kick out of seeing the place where the *real* Maria and the *real* Baron Von Trapp once lived and walked and presumably even sang—and so, to top it off, we gave in to their pleas and bought Maria's autobiography (the story, so the cover proclaims, that inspired the musical).

What we learned from the autobiography was that Maria's religion was even more important to her than the film lets on. Because (she says this, right in the book) after she fell in love with Captain Von

Trapp, she didn't just visit Mother Superior for a bit of sung advice about climbing every mountain and then make up her own mind, the way it happens in the musical. Oh, no. She went to visit Mother Superior and *asked her permission*. Not her advice, mind you, but her permission; Maria needed a yes or no.

The answer Maria received from Mother Superior took the following form: "We prayed to the Holy Ghost, and we held council, and it became clear to us . . . that it is the Will of God that you marry the Captain and be a good mother to his children." Did I say "permission"? This was virtually a command. Maria quotes her own nervous answer to the captain: "Th-they s-s-said I have to m-m-m-marry you-u!" Not *I can if I want to*—but *I have to*. And had Mother Superior refused permission, so Maria suggests, she would never have married the Captain, which would have meant no spine-tingling escape from Austria following the *Anschluss* [the union of Austria with Germany during World War II], no best-selling book, no singing career, no lodge in Vermont, no musical play, no Hollywood film. She would have had a different life altogether, all because of the decision (dare we say the whim?) of one individual, a religious leader, her Mother Superior.

Let us for a moment take Maria out of the mainstream and place her not in Roman Catholicism but in, say, the Unification Church; now imagine that the decision on whether she may marry the Captain rests in the hands not of Mother Superior but of the Reverend Sun Myung Moon [leader of the Unification Church]. All at once her decision to consult with her religious superior before marrying takes on a cast either sinister or amusing, depending on one's preferences. At that point, Maria Trapp believes *too* deeply; she becomes a weirdo.

Freud believed that deep religiosity was neurotic in nature, and many psychiatrists still do. Robert Coles, in his fine book *The Spiritual Life of Children,* relates his frustration during his training in psychiatry when a troubled young girl who was tormented by "bad habits" that could be controlled only through prayer never got around to doing what his teachers said she inevitably would—she never admitted that she was really talking about sex, not religion. Coles came to understand that religious commitments, whatever their characteristics, tend to be genuine expressions of human personality. Other therapists have not. That is why Stephen Arterburn and Jack Felton, in their 1991 book *Toxic Faith: Understanding and Overcoming Religious Addiction,* probably thought they were being progressive when they decided that some religious commitments were dysfunctional and others were just fine.

What would Arterburn and Felton have thought of Maria's decision to seek the permission of her religious leader before marrying the Captain? They do not tell us, exactly, but they do give us this account of some of the goings-on in one church's "toxic faith system": "The pastor, or shepherd as he was called, had final say in everything in the lives of his flock: whether to buy a house, take a vacation, get married, and even whom to marry." *Even whom to marry.* So if Maria really thought she could not marry without the approval of her Mother Superior, does that make the Catholic Church a kind of toxic faith itself, at least if people take it seriously?

America's discomfort, never slight, with religions that lie outside the mainstream seems to be at its zenith in matters touching procreation in general and marriage in particular. When the Supreme Court in 1879 sustained the authority of the state to prosecute Mormons for polygamy—which their religious doctrines allowed—one might suppose that the Justices were simply weighing the demands of religious freedom against the general regulatory power of the state. In fact, the Justices were reflecting the anti-Mormon fervor of the age, a fervor with religious roots and repressive results. Mormons, seen as blasphemers, were beaten and sometimes killed, their homes destroyed, their property stolen. Going off to Utah was of little help to the widely persecuted Mormons: "The West was no sanctuary," notes the historian Cushing Strout, "so long as Mormons persisted in their peculiarity." The Supreme Court understood perfectly well that the Mormons could not be permitted to be different. Even if it was required by religious belief, the Court wrote, the practice of polygamy was "subversive of good order." In other words, hatred of Mormons caused other people to act disorderly.

It has long been the American habit to be more suspicious of—and more repressive toward—religions that stand outside of the mainline Protestant–Roman Catholic–Jewish troika that dominates America's spiritual life. Even within the acceptable mainline, we often seem most comfortable with people whose religions consist of nothing but a few private sessions of worship and prayer, but who are too secularized to let their faiths influence the rest of the week. This attitude exerts pressure to treat religion as a hobby: one does not talk about one's faith and one does not follow the rules of one's faith if they cause behavior that the society considers immoral, such as polygamy, or actually dangerous, such as handling poisonous snakes. At that point, what has already been reduced to the level of hobby becomes even worse: "subversive of good order."

So, what does one do about the Mormons, Maria Trapp, and other people intoxicated by faith—people who not only refuse to keep quiet about their beliefs, but actually place the demands of their religions above the secular society's demands of "good order"? When mocking them doesn't work, we have another way to deal with them. In most of the world, it would be called kidnapping. In our media-dominated secular society, however, it is dressed up with the fancy name of "deprogramming." The tales are luridly familiar: child X is drawn into a religious cult, pressured, coerced, and brainwashed, loses the power of independent judgment, turns over all of her worldly possessions to the church, and works to draw in and brainwash others. What, other than a similar effort by those who love her, could possibly pull her free of the cult's influence?

For parents who watch in helpless pain as their children surrender free will to the regulation of some eccentric or repressive cult, the option of deprogramming must be attractive indeed. It takes a brainwashing, one might say, to undo a brainwashing. But just what is a cult? After all, Maria Trapp, well-known religious maniac who needed permission to marry, might be described as someone who has been drawn into a cult, even if her cult is a big and old and powerful one that does business under the name of the Roman Catholic Church. Roger Finke and Rodney Stark, in their 1992 book *The Churching of America, 1776–1990,* suggest defining a cult as a minority religion that is not a spinoff from a major religion. (The spinoffs, they say, are sects.) This definition carries no normative judgment. In popular usage, however, the term "cult" is used derisively. We envision something like the Branch Davidians, led by David Koresh, whose Waco, Texas, compound was the scene of a disastrous confrontation with law enforcement personnel early in 1993.

The psychiatrist Robert Jay Lifton, an expert on the problem of brainwashing and a critic of many cults but of deprogramming as well, argues that the cult problem "is best addressed educationally." According to Lifton, as public knowledge of cult tactics grows, "the elements of deception are less easy to maintain" and the decision on whether to enter a purported cult or not can therefore be a more informed one. And no matter how evil outsiders may think a cult to be, the more informed the choice to enter it, the less justification for interfering with that choice later. To Lifton's evident frustration, many deprogrammers have cited his work on brainwashing to justify the tactics that he deplores.

However, many of the people whose families wanted to deprogram them have a different view of matters. True, some of them recant after lengthy sessions with the deprogrammers (some have written sentimental accounts of the experience) but many others have refused to give up their new beliefs. Of those some have sworn out criminal or civil complaints against those to whom they refer as kidnappers. Although a number of jurisdictions have prosecuted deprogrammers for kidnapping their subjects, nearly all trials have ended in acquittals. (Several actions for civil damages against deprogrammers have apparently been successful.)

Obviously, there are psychologically damaging cults and, just as obviously, there are people whose religious piety is a cloak for some neurosis. The trouble is telling which are which. We seem too ready to assume that people who surrender to their religious leaders authority over matters that most of us prefer to decide for ourselves must be on the edge of at least temporary insanity, especially when the religious leaders are outside of the mainstream religions. When people begin to sign over wages and property, when they leave family and community behind, we too often judge them as not just religiously eccentric (which is problematic enough) but as members of a cult.

Moreover, there remains that nettlesome question of just who defines the mainstream. One might conclude that the distinction between cults and bona fide religions should be left to the experts, but it is not clear who the experts are. Mainstream denominations understandably have a bias in the matter, and they often support anticult literature and organizations. At the other extreme, it is not clear that psychiatrists, given the profession's historical antipathy toward religious devotion, are in the best position to judge.

But the distinction matters if one is to take seriously the problem of cults. In Margaret Atwood's powerful novel *The Handmaid's Tale,* some of the techniques practiced by today's deprogrammers are used to get Roman Catholic nuns to recant. Within the fiction, this is entirely consistent, for Atwood sketches a society in which holding to Catholicism in the face of secular punishment is seen by others as more than eccentric—even a bit maniacal. (They compare the nuns to witches.) The novel, of course, is only fiction, but Atwood intended it as a warning, insisting that every oppressive practice she describes has been used by some society. And one cannot help concluding that the society that tries to make members of unpopular religious groups renounce their views is, unhappily, our own.

Even if (as is certainly true) some cults are every bit as evil as the culture paints them, our mainstream antipathy toward the religions we call cults has gone a bit too far. Our tolerance for the practice of deprogramming supplies the evidence. We must not make the error of approving illegitimate means—kidnapping, psychological battering—because of the importance we attach to the end. Perhaps more imperative, we must resist the pressure to define what is outside of the mainstream, what is eccentric, as necessarily "subversive of good order." For unless one views the purpose of religion as making the mainstream comfortable, there will always be religious people—one hopes, lots of them—who are guided more by their faith than by the standards and demands of others, and who will therefore seem eccentric.

This brings us back to Maria Trapp. Had she grown up in today's America instead of Europe between the world wars, and had her religion not been Catholicism, perhaps she would never have gone to Mother Superior seeking permission to marry; more to the point, she might never have been a person of the sort who would go to Mother Superior for permission to marry. But if she had been the type to ask, and if she had done it, she would likely have been ridiculed for letting some religious leader control her personal life, much like the Western press poked fun at the 25,000 people who were married by the Reverend Sun Myung Moon. And if the ridicule did not persuade Maria to change, perhaps some well-meaning deprogrammer, hired by her worried parents, would have snatched her up and subjected her to psychological battering until she renounced her devotion to the eccentric, domineering Catholic cult. And this would have been sad, because it would have meant no book, no play, no film for our kids to enjoy.

And, incidentally, no religious freedom either.

A Religious Definition of "Cult"

Anne Husted Burleigh

> In the following selection, Anne Husted Burleigh points out that the Catholic *Catechism*, the summary of Catholic religious doctrine, defines the word "cult" simply to mean "worship," the act of individuals gathering together to praise God. Although the original sense of the word "cult" is positive, Burleigh explains, many people now associate "cult" with eccentric or even sinister quasi-religious movements. The result, she charges, is a fear of cults so strong that even legitimate religious movements have come under suspicion of being dangerous cults. She recommends that people carefully examine religious movements before labeling them with pejorative terms. Burleigh is a contributing editor for *Crisis*, a Catholic periodical that focuses on culture and politics.

Of the most basic words in our language, none has suffered more misunderstanding in our time than the word cult.

Originally cult—or *cultus*—meant worship, a gathering together to adore and give thanks to God. And so it still means in the Catholic *Catechism*, in which the term "cult" is immediately cross-referenced in the index to the term "worship."

To worship, to adore God is, according to the *Catechism*, "the first act of the virtue of religion." To adore God "is to acknowledge him as God, as the Creator and Savior, the Lord and Master of everything that exists, as infinite and merciful Love." This acknowledgment of the one God as Lord, which is worship or cult, "sets man free from turning in on himself, from the slavery of sin and the idolatry of the world."

Obviously, then, the Church defines cult in its original meaning of worship. The Church has always understood, as well, that from cult springs culture, the response of a people to the voice of God. Culture in turn may become a civilization, perhaps a great one. In any event, there is no living culture without roots in worship. Cutting off a culture from its religious origins in the cult saps the vitality of the culture—precisely the modern problem. When culture thus becomes divorced from authentic cult, then pseudo-cults arise.

Little wonder, consequently, that we Americans are confused by the severance of cult and culture. Alarmed by reports of satanic

Reprinted from Anne Husted Burleigh, "Cult: Catholic or Coercive?" *Crisis*, September 1997, by permission of *Crisis* magazine.

groups capturing gullible youth and gentle folk killing themselves in the hope of leaving their container bodies so as to sail away in the tail of a comet, we take cult to mean not worship of the one true God, but worship of an evil force. Although the Church understands cult to be worship in its primary and good sense, cult in the popular mind has become sinister, even deadly. To be sure, there are strange, spooky sects afoot these days, preaching doctrines and practices to unnerve any parent. As a result of the presence of eccentric, possibly dangerous sects, and as a result of our culture becoming unglued from true cult, the popular mind has developed a fear of cults so strong that even legitimate religious orders and movements such as Opus Dei, Legionaries of Christ, Focolare, and the Charismatic Movement are under suspicion of being cults of the sinister sort.

The cult stigma becomes difficult for these orders to combat, given the very nature of religious orders, which calls for discipline as part of their freely chosen way of life. Plagued, moreover, by our modern denial of authority, even authority freely recognized, and by our consequent disdain of discipline, religious orders and movements undergo yet more suspicion that they may be coercive cults.

Faced with the real danger of odd cults on the one hand, and the discipline of legitimate religious orders and movements on the other, how does one judge whether a movement is truly worshipful or whether it is false?

Jesus himself answers our dilemma. Cults and causes may be false; therefore judge them by their fruits.

"Beware of false prophets," he says, "who come to you disguised as sheep but underneath are ravenous wolves. You will be able to tell them by their fruits." He could not be more clear: "A sound tree produces good fruit but a rotten tree bad fruit. A sound tree cannot bear bad fruit, nor a rotten tree bear good fruit. Any tree that does not produce good fruit is cut down and thrown on the fire. I repeat, you will be able to tell them by their fruits."

To determine the soundness of a religious order or movement, we look for certain fruits in its members: love of Christ and his Church, expressed especially in reverence for the sacraments and in a prayer life modeled on traditional spiritual exercises; obedience to the authority of Scripture, the apostolic tradition, and the moral and doctrinal teachings of the Magisterium; absolute respect for the sacredness and freedom of the human person; and, finally, an emphasis on charity, prudence, and cheerfulness.

A further useful criterion for judging the truth of a movement is whether the members are mostly admirable and whether the order or movement seems to help or hinder their progress in all ways—spiritual, intellectual, moral, social.

As a final check on the authenticity of a movement, we look for its approval by the Vatican. To be certain, let the Church be our guide.

CHAPTER 5

PERSPECTIVES ON CULTS

SECRETS OF THE CULT

Mark Miller

In 1997, the Heaven's Gate cult made headlines when thirty-nine members committed suicide in an alleged attempt to reach heaven on the tail of a comet. Shortly before the mass suicide took place, one member, Rio DiAngelo, left the group in order to pursue a career opportunity. In the following selection, *Newsweek* reporter Mike Miller recounts DiAngelo's three-year odyssey inside the cult. Miller writes that DiAngelo describes his fellow cult members as gentle and fun-loving people. DiAngelo poignantly says, "I lost 39 of my closest brothers and sisters, my friends." However, he does believe that his friends succeeded in their attempt and that their souls live on in what he calls the "Next Level." DiAngelo also believes he remained behind because he was selected for a special task—to spread the message of Heaven's Gate now that his companions are gone.

For Rio DiAngelo, the first true premonition came last November. The members of Heaven's Gate had learned not to take their leader's predictions too literally, and their guru, Marshall Herff Applewhite, better known to his followers as "Do" was usually careful to hedge. But this time he seemed quite specific. The arrival of the comet Hale-Bopp was the sign they had been waiting for. The Earth would be "spaded over." The chariot would swing low in late March, when the comet burned brightest. Deliverance was near.

Along about January, Rio began to get a "disturbing feeling." DiAngelo, whose real name is Richard Ford, was a relative neophyte. Many members had been with Do since the 1970s; DiAngelo had arrived only three years before. He decided that he had to leave "the class," as he calls the group, because he "had a task to do." Perhaps sensing the end was near, he took a job at a Web-page design firm in the real world. He insists there was no plan for mass suicide. Still, he knew there was a "procedure" that would allow true believers to shed their "containers." He also knew that some members had gone to Mexico to buy phenobarbital, a barbiturate fatal in large doses.

DiAngelo was the last to leave before the others left for good. In eight hours of exclusive interviews with *Newsweek*, DiAngelo described his mind-bending three-year odyssey inside a cult obsessed with castration and the cosmos—and how he found the rotting bodies in a ritzy suburb of San Diego. DiAngelo, who considers himself a soul in an earthbound body ("my vehicle"), regards himself as a member, not an "ex-member," of Heaven's Gate, which he describes as "an advanced class for higher education," not a cult. "I lost 39 of my closest brothers and sisters, my friends," says DiAngelo. "And even though I'm trying to have control of this vehicle, it still disturbs me." DiAngelo hopes to join his brothers and sisters one day, though suicide, he hastens to add, "is not part of my plan."

First comes his moment of fame. DiAngelo is a living witness—to the repression and subtle mind control that permeated the suicide cult. His tale helps explain the eerie culture of Heaven's Gate, the lethal mix of New Age dreaming, extraordinary self-denial and sci-fi–soaked paranoia that led to the mass self-annihilation in Rancho Santa Fe. Last week DiAngelo sold the made-for-TV-movie rights to ABC (he won't say for how much) and this week he will be interviewed on "PrimeTime Live" by Diane Sawyer. He says he does not feel like a celebrity but rather "an instrument of clarification." He believes that his departed comrades would be "proud" of all the media hoopla. "They are laughing," says DiAngelo. "They really wanted the whole world to know this information but couldn't get it out. No one would listen. I think they would be happy."

Still, DiAngelo himself seems a little ambivalent about his own role. Returning to the world, he says, "was a slap in the face." On the other hand, he seemed to he enjoying himself as he ordered a big dinner (including wine) at a luxury hotel suite. What DiAngelo says is sometimes out of this world, but his manner is usually cool and self-contained. He learned from a master manipulator; he was molded by a regimen that made virtually every choice for its members, from their highest aspirations to their tastes in pop culture. Members of Heaven's Gate were allowed to watch TV—but they sat in assigned seats and were offered an odd blend of low- and highbrow fare. They loved "Star Trek." A PBS documentary on Thomas Jefferson was on the approved list; "GoldenEye," with Pierce Brosnan as Agent 007, was a no-no. If an actor or actress evoked sensuous feelings in a member of the "class," the class member was supposed to turn away.

Rio DiAngelo, or "Neody," as he was known within the group, is a seeker and a survivor. He drifted into the cult for the usual depressing reasons—broken family, bad relationships, a fascination with UFOs. But he escaped its final solution because he kept a sense of detachment and an instinct for self-preservation. He may be Do's "messenger," but he was never completely his pawn.

There is a story DiAngelo tells about his wretched childhood that is unintentionally revealing. He recalls his mother, whom he describes as violent and unstable, coming to hit him as a little boy. "You want to have this wonderful image of your mom, and all of a sudden, Mom turns into this rage. It's just like this doesn't look like Mom, this is somebody else." Most little boys would have cringed in horror. DiAngelo says he just laughed, or, as he put it, "the little vehicle would crack up, and that would make her even angrier, and she'd scream, 'Don't laugh at me!'"

DiAngelo refers to his childhood in southern California in the 1950s and '60s as "boot camp." His father walked out when he was 3, and he bounced back and forth between his grandmother's and his mother's care, if it can be called that. He was sent to various churches and schools, but never stayed long in any particular one. He became, not surprisingly, a searcher. He tried to be a hippie, a musician, an artist. He experimented with Eastern religion and read books on UFOs. He got married and had a child. Nothing filled the emptiness. Divorced, he drifted back home to live with his mother and her latest husband. He took strange pleasure in photographing their ashtrays, stacked high with old butts.

Then in January 1994, Rio, who had just turned 40, went to a hotel in Marina Del Rey to hear about a "last chance to advance beyond human." He listened as nine androgynous figures in loose clothes and short haircuts described the Earth as a "garden to grow souls to prepare them to advance to a higher level." Rio felt "an overwhelming desire, a compulsion to be part of this." He believed his true soul had matched with and entered his earthbound "vehicle." It was "like, OK, Monty, door number two, bam," recalled DiAngelo.

The only catch was that the cult wasn't taking new members. "They tried to talk me out of it," said DiAngelo. Two of the cult "overseers," "Srrody" and "Jwnody," told him the rules: no drinking, smoking or sex. Every member was "homeless by choice." Still, DiAngelo pleaded to be accepted. In the real world, as he put it, "I had nothing."

He did have an apartment in L.A. and a girlfriend, but he gave those up, along with his credit cards. There wasn't much of a bank account to worry about; business as a freelance scene painter was poor. Saying goodbye to his 11-year-old son, whom he had every other weekend, was harder. He explained that he was going off to learn how to get into heaven. "I think he understood," recalled DiAngelo, his eyes misting.

DiAngelo cut off his ponytail and shucked his name. Cult members are known by a three-letter prefix followed by "doti" or "ody" (a play on the founders, Do and Ti). DiAngelo picked "Neody" because "I felt new." Different names are chosen to deal with the outside world. Richard Ford became Rio DiAngelo—the river of angels. Neody hit the road with Srrody and Jwnody and the crew. "We went coast to coast. If it wasn't every state, it sure felt like it." Rising before dawn, handing out literature to skeptical earthlings, foraging for food, DiAngelo lost all sense of time. He finally found himself living in a warehouse in San

Clemente on the California coast. For about three months the group drank nothing but "master cleanser"—a concoction of lemonade, cayenne pepper and maple syrup—to rinse out their "vehicles" bloated by fast food. Then it was off to a Utah ski resort—bartering cooking and cleaning for room and board. Money was tight—funneled into the commune from odd jobs and the occasional trust-fund check.

DiAngelo heard "wonderful stories" about Do, their leader, but he did not actually see the sainted one until he had been in the cult for a month. One night, while they were camping in the desert outside Phoenix, Ariz., Do suddenly appeared in the light of the campfire, flanked by two disciples. "He was very security-minded," said DiAngelo. "With a lot of new students he had to be very careful." It was only a year after the Branch Davidians had died in the Waco conflagration, and Do feared that he was a target of the FBI. The leader often lived apart from his followers, though usually close by. DiAngelo was told that Do did not like the "vibrations" of new members who were "still trying to control their anger and the lusts."

"Getting control of the vehicle" was the goal of the class. At the Next Level, there is no gender. Thus it was necessary to "reprogram." The problem, as DiAngelo explains it, was that "the vehicle has a mind of its own." Sensuality "is the strongest addiction there is. It doesn't matter if it's male-female, female-female, male to male, female to dog. You think about it and it changes your whole vibration." Sexual partners weren't even necessary. "You can do it yourself, and you can do it for free."

DiAngelo says he gradually tamed his own sensual addiction, though "dreams are tough to control." But for others sexual temptation was too much. Before DiAngelo joined up, two members had quietly gone to Mexico to be castrated. The others increasingly talked about getting "neutered." Finally, about a year ago, Do himself decided to lead the way. "He did it to his own vehicle just to make sure. He protected us in every way," says DiAngelo. Do had trouble finding a doctor willing to perform the operation, however; most wanted him to see a psychiatrist. The one he got "goofed," as DiAngelo put it. Do healed very slowly. Still, five others eagerly followed. "They couldn't stop smiling and giggling," says DiAngelo. "They were excited about it."

DiAngelo chose not to follow his master's example. "Everything is freedom of choice," he explained. "It's very rights-oriented." Under the strict regimen of the cult, however, members did not have many choices to make. Most decisions were made by the cult's hierarchy. At the top—in heaven—there was Ti, the former nurse and astrologer Bonnie Nettles, who had run off with Do in the 1970s and ascended to a Higher Level in 1985 after her vehicle was broken by liver cancer. Cult members believe her mind was so powerful it "short-circuited her vehicle." Do would have celestial conversations with Ti, about everything from the daily chores to the group's ultimate destination. Do in turn would pass messages on to the "overseers"—a cadre of longtime cult members—who would instruct the class. Members did nothing alone; each had a "check partner" to guard against backsliding.

There were "procedures" for everything, meticulously recorded in longhand in a three-ring binder. "If you needed something," DiAngelo said, "you wouldn't go to the store. You'd write the Individual Needs Department." To guard against overweening pride and self-confidence, members were taught to be conditional in their language. The proper way to approach the "overseer" for "individual needs" was: "I may be wrong, but it seems that my deodorant is running out."

By the time DiAngelo arrived, Do had abandoned his cruder mind-control games. Followers were no longer required to report to head-quarters every 12 minutes around the clock or to wear helmets (exhaustion set in, and the headgear was too hot). Still, there was always a "sense of urgency" about becoming "nonhuman" because there was no telling when the spaceship would arrive to take them all away. "You can't be thinking like a human, you can't be thinking are you going to have sex or you've got to shave or you have angry thoughts or raging hormones. You've got to be ready."

But ready for what, exactly? The precise method of departure was the source of some confusion. It was clear that Earth was becoming increasingly inhospitable. The messages posted by Heaven's Gate on the Internet were being greeted by scorn and derision. Do was fearful that the Feds might attack at any moment. For a time, he seemed to welcome a final showdown. On the video shelf next to "The Sound of Music" were conspiracy-theory videos about Waco and the IRS. In 1995, the cult built a fortress with cement and old tires in the New Mexico desert and bought weapons—at least five handguns and two rifles with sniper scopes. A few members who knew how to handle guns tried to teach the others how to shoot, but the enthusiasm for gunplay, and perhaps the skill level, was low among Do's gentle flock. Do himself finally received a message from Ti indicating that a shootout with the Luciferians was not the right Last Exit.

How then to reach the Higher Level? There was always the promise and hope of the spaceship's swooping down from heaven. From time to time, the group would go out into the middle of the desert and stay until dark, "just kind of hoping and praying that Ti would know we were here, and come and get us," says DiAngelo. Some would be dis-appointed when the heavens stared back blankly, but for most, the seances were "fun," says DiAngelo.

Sex may have been forbidden, but fun was not. "We loved having a good time and would have a good time as often as possible." Heaven's Gate was full of "fun-loving people, very flexible and open-minded." There were expeditions to UFO museums and the movies—carefully chosen by Do, of course—and, from time to time, feasts. While sex wasn't essential to the vehicle, eating ("consuming") was. So why not enjoy a little cake and ice cream? (San Diego police found seven quarts of Starbuck's Java Chip ice cream in the refrigerator of the so-called Mansion of Death.)

As Hale-Bopp drew closer last winter, the class seemed to have more and more fun. By now the group had settled into the villa in Rancho Santa Fe and begun to earn good money from cyberspace as Web-page designers. In late February, the entire class traveled to Las Vegas and stayed in the Stratosphere Hotel. They went to Cirque du Soleil and carefully recorded their winnings at the slot machines and gaming tables ($58.91), as well as the money spent on water ($2.28) and on tickets for rides, including a free-fall contraption called the Big Shot ($123). In the weeks to come, there would be trips to Sea World and to see "Star Wars."

But by then, DiAngelo's "disturbing feeling" had prodded him to directly approach Do, something he had never done before. Members could communicate with Do only in writing; DiAngelo asked for a private meeting. "I told him I felt I had something to do outside the class, like a task." He told Do that he "didn't want to leave the class at all," but that he had been offered a full-time job on the outside working for InterAct Entertainment, a company that often used Higher Source, the cult's Web-page design outfit. After reflection, Do summoned DiAngelo. "He told me that he had talked to Ti just now, and he felt like it might be part of a plan, and that I didn't understand and that he didn't understand." There was an inkling, however. DiAngelo had been chosen earlier to write a film script about the group's story. He had been volunteered by his partner, Otis Paceman (a play on "Oti Spaceman"), because of his experience in "the film industry" (which was limited mostly to building props for a theme park). Later, DiAngelo would realize that he had been sent forth to tell the story of Heaven's Gate.

DiAngelo insists he had no real foreboding of mass suicide. Do talked of his followers' "leaving their vehicles"—but only by their own choice. Do himself would never give the order. Naturally, said DiAngelo, no one wanted to be left behind if Do himself exited. "It's like you didn't want to go anyplace without your dad," he said.

Out on his own, DiAngelo stayed in touch with the group by e-mail. But on the Monday after Palm Sunday, his messages vanished into a void, which he found "odd." Then on Tuesday, he received a FedEx package at work. He says he knew instantly who the package was from—and what had happened. Curiously, he didn't open the package until he had returned home that evening. One glance at the letter within confirmed his suspicions: "By the time you read this, we will have exited our vehicles," it read.

In the morning he matter-of-factly announced to his boss, Nick Matzorkis, that the cult members were dead. Not quite believing him, Matzorkis drove DiAngelo to the house in Rancho Santa Fe. DiAngelo had come prepared. He took out a bottle of cologne, splashed it on a shirt, and held it over his nose. Still, "the smell could knock you over," he said. There were his "brothers and sisters," or at least their abandoned vehicles, lying peacefully in their Nikes beneath the purple shrouds. Their bags were packed with clothes and other essentials, including lip balm, and their pockets were filled with $5 bills and rolls of quarters. Ever since a member of the cult had been hassled by police for vagrancy, the "monks," as they called themselves to outsiders, carried money and IDs. "It was spooky and weird," says DiAngelo, who had brought a video camera "to keep the facts accurate."

Their deaths were "not suicide," says DiAngelo, because their souls live on at the Next Level. He has "no doubt" that everyone went "on their own." As for him, "I don't think I'm ready to make that leap right now. I would like to go to the Next Level but quite frankly I don't think I'm ready yet." Had he stayed in the "class," he says he would have declined to "exit his vehicle."

Though he is the last insider, Rio DiAngelo is not the only survivor. A man who goes by the name of "Rkk" told *Newsweek* that he, too, had received a FedEx package containing master tapes of Do's farewell message and the goodbyes of his former "crew mates." Rkk describes himself as the cult's prodigal son. For more than 20 years, he floated in and out of the class, leaving when he could not master his sexual urges. He quit at the end of last year ("I didn't get the control of my vehicle that was required to stay") but stayed in touch via e-mail. Rkk says he would have gone through with the suicide "in a microsecond. I'm tired of this stupid planet. I don't know how my exit's going to happen, but I hope it happens soon."

DiAngelo has more temporal desires. In addition to "demystifying" the cult for the media, he says he and InterAct have been "entrusted" with the Higher Source Website company. He wants to "preserve the dignity and quality that they had always provided." He added that he would "welcome new clients." He has long since lost touch with his mother and his siblings; his ex-wife, he says, reminded him of his mother. His son is a different matter. At the beginning of last week, DiAngelo told a friend that he didn't plan to see his son, who was the child of his "vehicle," not him. But by midweek in his interview with *Newsweek*, he seemed to be wavering, and by Friday, after talking to his lawyer, he said that he did plan to "see the child of the vehicle."

Then there is DiAngelo's old girlfriend. Desperate after his 1988 divorce, DiAngelo had tried a "very-high-class dating service." He met someone with "style, class and beauty." He was "kind of thrown by this feeling, like, 'Gee, is this really the one?'" The two had problems, but, says DiAngelo, "the vehicle is still in love with this woman today." Will he call? He "hopes to talk to her," he said. There are many roads to heaven's gate.

INSIDE THE BRANCH DAVIDIANS

Alice Scott

In 1989, twenty-six-year-old Robert Scott moved from Colorado to California, where he joined a group of spiritual disciples led by the self-appointed prophet David Koresh. In 1993, the FBI lay siege to Koresh's Texas compound in an attempt to arrest Koresh for alleged wrongdoings, including stockpiling illegal weapons. More than eighty people died in the ensuing fifty-one-day stand-off. Robert, however, was spared this grim fate: After only nine months with the group, he had become so paranoid and delusional that Koresh had ordered the young man home. In an effort to understand her son's fragile mental condition upon his return, Alice Scott launched an investigation of David Koresh and his teachings, as well as of cults in general. Her efforts culminated in the publication of a book, *The Incredible Power of Cults: Hard Facts on the Soft Persuaders.* In the following excerpt, Scott recounts her son's experiences with David Koresh and his followers, the Branch Davidians.

When self-appointed prophet David Koresh led his followers to a stand-off with federal agents in Waco, Texas in 1993, a nation watched in disbelief. How far would 85 people go to defend their seemingly insane "savior," their fabricated belief structure, and a hollow "message of salvation?"

Fifty-one days later we learned the incredible answer. On Monday, April 19, 1993, in a spectacular fireburst, the Waco compound exploded killing David Koresh and his 85 followers, including 17 children.

As I witnessed the brilliant and thunderous explosions on television with my son Robert, a large part of me seemed to be taken away with the smoke. I felt I had known David Koresh from the many conversations we had on the phone. I had read letters my son shared with me from [his friend] Jimmy Riddle and others who died in the fire. I thought about the 17 children, who in their innocence, were offered no choice but to die. How could it happen? I asked my son for explanations.

"Did you *really* believe David Koresh was Jesus Christ?" I asked.

"Yes."

"Do you mean that if you had not been sent home when you were, that you would have followed David Koresh and the others into death?"

My son stared at me with his large, determined brown eyes. "I would have killed for him. I would have died for him. I didn't want to leave, and if I hadn't been sent home, I would have been reincarnated with him now."

I couldn't understand, but I believed my son. And as I watched the images on television settle to ashes, I vowed to learn about the incredible power that cults and cult leaders have over their followers. I asked Robert to help me understand.

The Spring of 1989

When Robert arrived in California, his head was filled with great expectations. With three years of military service behind him and a technical degree in hand, he had his first job since graduating as an avionics technician. He shared a mobile home with two others, 1200 miles away from family and friends. He was wide-eyed, ambitious and hopeful. I could tell by his letters and phone calls that he was applying the same dedication on the job that he had put into his studies. He was determined to learn, to understand, and to apply his talents.

But life does not unfold with the promise and predictability of a textbook. After six months, Robert's company began downsizing and he was laid off. Other aviation firms where he applied for work were going through the same economic throes. Meanwhile, after his roommates stole many of his personal effects, he turned to temporary housing at a shelter provided by the church he was attending.

One afternoon, while Robert was doing his laundry, Jimmy Riddle happened into the same laundromat and the two friends renewed their camaraderie. Jimmy was working as a custodian at the avionics firm adjacent to Robert's former employer. Robert enjoyed Jimmy's bright banter, his understanding of Robert's situation and his genuine warmth and concern. Jimmy had always impressed him by his cheerfulness and dedication on the job, and now Jimmy reached out his hand in aid.

Robert still felt a bit envious of Jimmy, remembering an earlier conversation in which Jimmy had mentioned planning to take some vacation time to go on a religious retreat in Texas. "People from all over the world will be there to study the Bible," Jimmy said. Robert asked about the retreat. Sensing that Robert might be interested in the religious group, Jimmy invited him to his house to meet other members of his "adopted family."

The "Family" Home

At the house, Robert was introduced to Steve Schneider, a man in his middle thirties, blond, and with a very friendly personality that immediately instills respect and trust. Steve explained to Robert that the Bible was now harmonized, that the Old and New Testaments were now in agreement. Intrigued by this possibility, Robert wanted to learn more.

Over the next few weeks, Robert accepted several invitations to return to the "family" home to discuss the Bible. On his second visit, he was instructed by Sherry Jewell, a former school teacher who told stories from the Bible in a very understandable, mesmerizing manner. She, too, was very open and friendly, and Robert immediately felt a rapport with her and her attractive daughter.

On his third visit, Robert met a small group of people who sat in a circle in the living room of the stone house, listening to the various speakers give interpretations of lessons from the Bible.

On his fourth visit, Robert met David Koresh (at that time he was still known as Vernon Howell), who talked to him one-on-one about the Bible. David would ask Robert to quote anything he wanted from the Bible. Robert would open his book and begin reading when David would interrupt him, finishing the Bible verses from memory, and give his interpretation. Robert was very impressed by the man's knowledge and ease with the teachings of the Bible.

Needing to find a more permanent place to stay, and feeling a kinship with this very special group of people who shared his love of the Bible, Robert asked if they had room for him to stay at the house. David Koresh seemed taken by surprise and told Robert that he wasn't running a boarding house. Robert laughed and reiterated his desire to be a part of the group. David told him that he must accept his teachings, Robert agreed, and the group welcomed him into their home.

Living with the Group

Conditions were crowded at the house. Robert took his sleeping bag, backpack, and a small metal locker, and camped out on the dirt floor of the musty, drafty garage behind the house. It was the men's dormitory where, over the next several weeks, as many as twenty men at a time were resident. Jimmy Riddle slept in the camper shell of his pickup truck, parked next to the garage. The women made accommodations in the house. David Koresh, when he was in town, stayed in the house.

Because of the large number of people living so closely together, strict rules and regulations were followed. Individuals were allotted time segments in which to use bathroom facilities, especially during the rush hours in the morning, but there never seemed to be any problems or conflicts.

Occupants were assigned chores, which insured that the bathroom, as well as the rest of the house, was always clean. Meals were prepared and the dishes were washed. It was, indeed, one very large, happy and well-organized family. Robert felt fortunate to be accepted by this warm and very caring group of people.

Soon Robert found a job at another avionics firm and was able to contribute his share to the upkeep of the house and for his food. But working became secondary. Learning and understanding the teachings of David Koresh gradually consumed Robert's interest, as it had with those he lived with.

There was a schedule for everything except for David's teachings. When inspiration touched him, David would assemble everyone in the living room for a Bible session. Sometimes the sessions would last a few minutes, sometimes they would go on for hours. They could occur during the day, which required that everyone not away at work drop the chores they were doing to listen to him; they could occur in the middle of the night, at which time everyone would be awakened to attend the session.

At all times, David Koresh was in total control. He was always informal, sometimes standing and delivering a dramatic story from the Bible, sometimes sitting on the floor and playing with his feet or eating a sandwich and quoting from the Bible and giving his interpretation. Sometimes he strummed his guitar, putting together a special message into the form of a song. Always, he held everyone's attention and spoke with a divine wisdom and knowledge. Using his own words, everyone considered him the "Lamb of Revelation." Robert knew he was in the privileged company of someone special.

A Failed Mission

Robert knew that he was special too. Soon after his arrival at the house, David Koresh singled Robert out to accompany him on a spiritual mission. Robert cleaned up and shaved while David had his hair braided by Sherry Jewell. David Koresh got out the motorcycle, Robert climbed aboard behind him and the two were off on their mission.

They called on a young couple who were members of the Seventh Day Adventist church, the denomination David preferred to recruit from. With Robert sitting to his right and the couple seated directly across from him, David proceeded to read from the Bible and give his interpretation. The young couple seemed genuinely interested, following in their own well-marked Bible, but after two hours Robert began to nod off. David admonished him for not being ready to accept his teachings and they left shortly after.

Robert recalls that after they returned to the house, everyone was disappointed for the young couple. They had chosen not to accept David's teachings and the group expressed concern for their souls being lost. And it was then that Robert learned that his "job" during the recruiting mission was to act enthusiastic in an effort to stir an emotional positive reaction from the couple. He was never asked to go on another mission.

For two weeks, Robert went to work, did his chores at the house, and listened to David Koresh preach, but no matter how hard he tried, he never totally grasped the message or understood the points David was trying to make. He was always persuaded to take his time, to keep an open mind, to concentrate on David's words, and that eventually it would all come together for him "when the time is right."

Meanwhile, David would hold review sessions in which he sped through lesson after lesson, exhilarating everyone. No one was allowed to interrupt him with questions. If the meaning wasn't clear, it would become clear later. "Take it by faith now; you'll see later. Just concentrate and listen. Soon enough you will learn," David would say. Determined to get the message, Robert spent all his free time reviewing phrases and concentrating on David's words. At night he would fall asleep, concentrating on receiving the light.

Suddenly, one day it happened. It all became clear to Robert. David had been reading from the Book of Revelations about a man named Faithful and True who was riding a white horse. The man's eyes were as a flame of fire and on his head were many crowns. Koresh told his followers that that man was holding up a Bible in his right hand and his name was Christ. He then asked them to close their eyes and follow along with the vision that he, David, had, and he continued to describe Christ on the white horse. Then he asked them to open their eyes.

"That describes me, doesn't it?" David asked. "I am the man riding that white horse and I'm holding the Bible in my right hand. You believe it, don't you? You do see it with your own eyes, don't you?"

And Robert saw. He understood the true meaning of the messages. He was feeling exhilarated and true acceptance into the group, for finally he understood what everyone else knew—David Koresh was Jesus Christ! The revelation was incredibly powerful.

Life Inside the Cult

For the next several weeks, Robert fell into the routine of work, chores, instruction and sleep. But life was different now because he had a strong sense of direction and meaning. He was able to share his new purpose on earth with teachers, engineers, lawyers, nurses, former pastors, construction workers and janitors, all followers of David Koresh. They ranged in age from the teens to the sixties, making it a multi-generational family. But all was not well in paradise.

David Koresh was always the final authority in every matter, and because of his spiritual nature, was never questioned publicly. But following in his footsteps was very difficult. David would treat his followers like small children, freely giving reprimands much like an insensitive parent, "You know better than that, now don't you? What's going on in your head? What do you have for brains, spaghetti?" Inside, his followers cowered.

But the study sessions continued, sometimes lasting as many as eighteen hours without stop, yet no one left or complained. Literally, they were under his spell, anticipating and accepting every word as if in a state of hypnotic acceptance. During those times between lectures, most cult members felt an addictive need for another "fix" of inspirational teaching.

But was this a cult? Robert remembers many occasions where members joked and laughed at the mere suggestion. This immediately threw suspicion off and he dismissed his own concerns as foolish. Besides, there were no obvious signs of cult activity. For instance, he was not asked to give all his money and possessions to the group (although later he could not recall what he did with his paychecks, or whether or not he even had a bank account. This part of his life in the cult seemed to be erased, in his words, "because money and material things were unimportant to us.")

Also, members were free to leave the group, and many did. But those who stayed became stronger and stronger in their convictions.

Dietary Restrictions

David Koresh developed much of his mind control over his followers by establishing a strict dietary regimen. By quoting and interpreting scriptures, he was able to convince his followers that certain foods were unclean, such as red meats (especially pork) and foods commercially prepared with chemicals and additives. So the Branch Davidian diet was deficient in animal proteins and high in carbohydrates.

Forbidden were such foods as pork, shrimp, chocolate, coffee, regular tea, cakes and sodas. Rarely did they have beef or any animal products. Instead, meals were prepared with fresh fruits, limited amounts of vegetables, poultry and breads. Turkey hot dogs were a common favorite. Popcorn was served regularly, especially after long study sessions. Sometimes it was the only food available on a given day. Other times, just popcorn and fruit.

But to keep his followers off balance and dependent on his "wisdom," David Koresh added other food restrictions. Liquids, including water, were not allowed at meals. And certain foods could not be eaten together. For instance, oranges could be eaten with grapes but not with raisins. Fruit could not be eaten with vegetables unless the vegetable was freshly cooked corn or the fruits were lemons, pineapples or avocados. Apples could be eaten with vegetables if they were stewed first, as Koresh believed that the chemistry of the apple changed when cooked.

Men were sometimes allowed to drink beer, but only certain brands, and no more than two spaced one hour apart.

Vitamins and dietary supplements were not allowed.

Certain members were assigned the chore of preparing the food. They even prepared sack lunches for those who worked regular jobs. Take-out lunches usually included fruit and turkey hot dogs or a vegetable patty. One member blended the tea from herbs and tea leaves kept in plastic bags in the kitchen.

David Koresh did not follow his own dietary regimen, however. He was put on this earth, he would explain, to experience and suffer all the sins of the world (which included the sin of eating unhealthy foods) so that when he stood in judgment of sinners on Judgment Day, he would have "experience of all sin and degradation on earth." Consequently, he would sometimes savor a large bowl of ice cream in front of a group of followers, telling them to give thanks to him for taking on their sins while they remained pure and clean.

Life in the Branch Davidian house was without outside influence. Radios, television, newspapers and magazines were forbidden (except for David Koresh, of course). The members were "protected" from the "lies and evils of the outside world." (It wasn't until my son came home that he found out that the Berlin Wall had come down several months before.) Instead, David would often show selected movies, and each would have a message. Most were "R" rated or war movies; few depicted life as it really is. Koresh used the movie plots to show his followers that they were just like the underdogs in the stories, and that through his leadership they would be victorious in the end, receiving power, status and salvation.

Members were also encouraged to exercise; the women often did aerobics, while the men engaged in weight lifting.

The Waco Compound

After several weeks in California, Robert was invited to join other members in the group travelling to Waco, Texas, for two weeks of intensive training and "gathering for atonement."

Mt. Carmel was located on 77 acres several miles from Waco. It was very active with a great deal of construction underway. But Robert's schedule was set for intense instruction, which he received from David Koresh's parents.

David Koresh arrived the second week and took over the training, which filled every day.

It was during this time that Robert first overheard references to "Branch Davidians," although he was told personally that the group was not affiliated with any organized religion.

It was also during this time that Robert heard about "special studies" being given privately by David Koresh in his bedroom, or "the upper room" as he called it. In his naiveté, Robert hoped he would be chosen for a special study—others often waited hours for them.

He later realized what was happening when David Koresh announced in a "new light" revelation that all women belonged to him and him alone. From that moment on all men were to remain celibate. Husbands were to turn their wives over to David and receive their own "perfect wives" in heaven. There was no longer a need to be married while on earth.

This was another "last straw," which caused several couples to leave the group. Steve Schneider was one who found the teaching unbelievable. To get him to stay, David "anointed" Steve to a special position and gave him additional responsibilities. And after many persuasive talks, David convinced Steve and his wife to remain under the revised rules. As a result, their faith became even stronger.

Robert, meanwhile, spent all his free time concentrating on David's message, trying to understand what he was teaching, trying to be worthy so that understanding would come. He would hear David's voice over and over in his head. The more he tried to make sense out of David's messages, the more muddled he became.

He took long walks along the many trails at the compound, meditating on "the word," concentrating on David's teaching. On one of these walks, during a period of intense concentration, "my mind opened up and all of a sudden a million different thoughts came in at one time, kwish, right into my head. I guess it was bad stuff because it wasn't a fun experience. But I tried to look at it logically and try to think, 'What is this? What is happening to my mind?' And not being able to understand what is going on is what really made it hard."

Escape from the Branch Davidians

Robert's episode in Waco was the beginning of his mental trauma. He began sensing an invisible entity trying to kill him.

"At first it was trying to get me to kill myself, to do it voluntarily through delusions. Not physically, but mentally kill myself, like no longer breathing, or just willfully stopping the heart. It was totally beyond anything I had ever felt before. And it was beyond scary, it was terrifying. And I couldn't fight it because it wasn't something outside, it was something inside me that was trying to do this."

In his terror, Robert would panic and seek out others, hugging them and pouring out his grief. But others offered little or no consolation.

Eventually, Robert felt that the invisible "entity" would do the killing, but only at the time of its choosing. Meanwhile, it would constantly stalk him.

"I acted like, and I felt like, I was a person about to be killed. It had the ability to just stop my life. And it was beyond my control, often coming to me when I was about to fall asleep, then backing away again when I was wide awake. I constantly felt the hand of death on me."

After Robert was returned to California, he began hallucinating, seeing the world change into the Garden of Eden, which David Koresh promised it would, only to have it return to the "evil world of reality" before he could step out of it. Or laser beams would blast out from unexpected sources, aimed at severing his penis and splitting him into two sexless beings. And God lived beyond Uranus, waiting for events on earth to complete their designed course.

It was then that Robert was sent home to us to recover.

Conversations with Koresh

During the 3½ years it took for Robert to completely recover, I had several conversations with David Koresh. I felt that if I knew more about the group and the man that Robert was involved with, I could better help him recover.

The phone calls I made to David resulted more in frustration than resolve.

First of all, I never had the opportunity to talk to someone other than David. If someone else answered the phone, the second voice I would hear would always be David's. He would not tell me who else was in the group or if any others had suffered the same hallucinations that Robert had. He refused to talk about himself. He did state that the group was "not associated with any Christian organization," and it had no formal name. "We're just a bunch of young men who meet together occasionally for Bible study," he said.

David always talked to me in a very rapid-fire manner, and very quickly he would manipulate the conversation to talking about his "revelation knowledge," which I never could understand. He tried to convince me that he had the "truth" about God's word and that everything I had been taught all my life was a lie. He would not help me understand Robert's condition, how he got that way, or how he might be helped.

Although the talks with David Koresh did little in helping me with Robert's recovery, they did help me understand the man, his influence and his control.

During the 51-day standoff in Waco, Texas between the Branch Davidians and the federal agents of the Bureau of Alcohol, Tobacco and Firearms (ATF), I felt I understood exactly what David Koresh was doing. The gentle but firm voice talking in circles was all too familiar to me. I know he relished the power of keeping the ATF at bay, wondering what his next move would be. And in a very real sense, he was controlling the FBI, the President of the United States, and the entire nation because he commanded the attention of the media. And I could almost hear him talking to his followers: "See, I told you they (the ATF) would do this, didn't I? They are exactly as I described them, aren't they? Now you believe I am who I say I am, don't you? They are the evil of the world, they have come to destroy us, and we shall triumph beyond the apocalypse!"

I was saddened for those who fell under his power and control.

My heart goes out to those federal agents who were killed or injured and their families and friends. I continue to grieve for everyone who died in the fire, but even more I grieve for those who survived the fire and are still caught up in the spiritual deception.

LIFE AFTER MASS UNIFICATION

Melinda Henneberger

The Unification Church was founded by Reverend Sun Myung Moon in Korea in the late 1950s. Moon and his converts, typically called Moonies, expanded to the United States shortly thereafter. In 1982, Moon performed a mass wedding at Madison Square Garden in New York City that included more than two thousand couples who, following Unification tradition, were matched with one another by Moon himself. In the following selection, *New York Times* writer Melinda Henneberger reports on a number of Moon's followers who took part in the 1982 wedding ceremony. Henneberger focuses on Jonathan and Debby Gullery, describing their decision to enter into an arranged marriage, their continuing devotion to the church, and their ongoing role as Unification parents and church members. However, Henneberger also relates the negative experiences of some of the other marriage participants, who have since left the Unification Church.

When Jonathan and Debby Gullery were married in 1982, in a mass wedding of 2,075 couples at Madison Square Garden, they were widely viewed as bit players in a bizarre show produced by the Rev. Sun Myung Moon. Strangers screamed at them as they sold flowers on the street, and Mrs. Gullery's father said he thought seriously about having her kidnapped and brought home.

But ten years later, the Gullerys say, both they and their church have grown up and settled down. On a recent evening, amid the chaos of bedtime for their three young children, they took turns coaxing the 4-year-old back to her room while Mrs. Gullery's father, who was visiting from Vermont, took refuge in the novel he was reading in the living room of their suburban home.

Mr. Gullery now owns his own graphic arts business, and the couple's oldest child, who is 7, attends the local public school. Their youngest is 2. To celebrate their 10th anniversary, they took the children to Burger King.

"Things change in 10 years," Mrs. Gullery said. "Our church has changed, we've changed, our family has changed. With our neighbors, we didn't put a sign out and say, 'Here we are, we're the neighborhood Moonies,' but they all have kids and after they got to know us, it was O.K. The last couple of years have been fairly low key."

Their lives are nonetheless quite different from their neighbors'. They remain completely dedicated to the Unification Church, rising early each morning for family prayer, and offering up all their daily tasks to the service of God and Mr. Moon, who is for them the second Messiah.

They see their job as Unificationist parents as integral to the world's redemption. Both do work for the church and socialize principally with other church members in Westchester County, New York. The county has the nation's largest concentration of Unificationists, according to church officials, because Mr. Moon himself lives in Tarrytown, New York.

The Gullerys defer to Mr. Moon in matters large and small, saying they are like early Christians privileged to live in their master's time and have the benefit of his counsel.

But they also have worked hard to gain acceptance in their community, and are eager to talk about their lives.

Seated at their dining room table, along with a church spokesman whose presence was a condition of all interviews with Unificationist families, they described their decision to allow Mr. Moon to arrange their marriage as a great relief.

"It was comforting to me because I'd made a lot of mistakes in my life," said Mr. Gullery, 38, a former newspaper reporter from New Zealand. "Feelings can change in a week or a month, and then there's nothing left."

Mrs. Gullery, also 38, who is from Canada, said she was mourning the end of the hippie era and living with friends in a teepee on Vancouver Island before she joined the church in 1977.

In the Unification tradition, romantic liaisons are forbidden until the members are deemed by Mr. Moon to be spiritually ready to be matched at a huge gathering where he points future spouses out to one another. His followers believe that his decisions are based on his ability to discern their suitability and see their future descendants. Many are matched with people of other races and nationalities, in keeping with Mr. Moon's ideal of unifying all races and nations in the Unification Church.

Though some couples are matched immediately before the mass wedding ceremonies, which are held every two or three years, most have long engagements during which they are typically posted in different cities or even continents, and get to know one another through letters.

The Gullerys were engaged for 18 months before their marriage on July 1, 1982, but were apart for most of that time. "I spent the time praying a lot—I don't know what you did," Mrs. Gullery said playfully to her husband, throwing the cap of a jug of apple cider across the table at him.

The wedding, they say, was a day to remember, with all 2,075 brides and grooms in identical outfits, filling the arena's floor. It was the first mass wedding performed by Mr. Moon, and there have since been even larger ceremonies in Korea.

After the wedding, the Gullerys were separated again for another two years, until Mr. Moon felt they were spiritually ready to consummate the marriage.

"You need time to make a relationship, and many couples do missionary work for a while," Mrs. Gullery explained. Her family thought it odd when she and her husband slept in separate bedrooms on their first visit home, she said, but they saw the waiting period as an important period of "heavenly dating."

In Mr. Moon's view, marriage is based on commitment to the church as much as to the other person, and love comes later, through shared ideals.

Hye Yong Hendricks, of Irvington, New York, who was also married in the mass wedding at Madison Square Garden, said her love for her husband, Tyler, has grown steadily, calmly, out of enormous respect. In answer to a question, she said she was not familiar with the concept of romantic love.

"You know, Romeo and Juliet," said her husband, trying to help.

Love and Mismatches

Karen and Kevin Smith, of Mamaroneck, New York, on the other hand, almost giddily described being "completely and totally in love" by the time they began living together, four years after their wedding. Mrs. Smith said, laughing, that the two "met across a crowded room," and her husband chimed in something about "their intimate garden wedding" at Madison Square.

Of course, not every couple married on that day in July did grow to love each other. A former church member living in Arlington, Va., said she was married to a man who told her from the outset that he was gay, did not even like her, and married her only so he could have children in the church. When she complained to church leaders, she said they responded that she should pray and strengthen her faith.

Gordon Newfeld, of Vancouver, said he had always had trouble forming relationships and was drawn to the Unificationists in large part by the prospect of an arranged marriage. He left the church because he was never allowed to live with the woman he married at Madison Square Garden. For two years, he lived in the United States while his wife lived in France, where she eventually fell in love with another man and left the church, he said.

"Then I spent another two years waiting to be rematched until I finally said, 'To heck with this, I don't want to wait anymore'," said Mr. Newfield who now views the time that Unificationists are asked to wait before living together as "just a sneaky way to keep you working for the church."

The church spokesman, Peter Ross, said that only 5 to 10 percent of the couples married at Madison Square Garden had divorced, and that most of those had left the church; divorce within the church is not normally allowed. Though church critics say the divorce rate is actually several times that, none can give an authoritative figure.

To those who do make it through the waiting period before a couple is allowed to live together, Mr. Moon offers guidelines on how the marriage is to be consummated, through a three-day ritual that involves prayer, a ceremonial bath with a handkerchief given to the couple on the day of their wedding, and explicit instructions about sexual positions. The symbolic ceremony is intended to purify the sexual act tainted by the sin of Adam and Eve, who the church believes caused the fall of man by having intercourse before they were spiritually mature.

Despite the group's dim view of what they call Hollywood-style romance, Mr. Moon does not shy away from endorsing conjugal enjoyment.

"Reverend Moon is pretty graphic sometimes," said Mr. Ross, the church spokesman. "Reverend Moon says when man and woman come together the cosmos should resound."

Unificationists are encouraged to have as many children as possible. Long after the wedding, the Gullerys finally arranged to take a honeymoon, at a country inn in Connecticut; by then, Mrs. Gullery was seven months' pregnant.

As the couple looked back on the day that Mr. Moon chose them for one another a dozen years ago, Mrs. Gullery's father, Peter Dicenso, who had joined them at the table, interrupted.

"I could do the same thing," he said of Mr. Moon's process of walking around a crowded room and pointing couples out to one another. "You have him on a pedestal too high—more than the Pope or the Archbishop of Canterbury. I love both of you very much," he said, shaking his head, "but I still don't have much faith in him."

Mr. Dicenso said he now accepted his daughter's choice, and added that he has to admit he has never seen a more loving home. But he worried aloud about whether his grandchildren would be stigmatized, and could not resist reminding his daughter of her early years in the church, when they were largely estranged.

"You didn't have to run away," he told her, smiling, but clearly speaking from his heart. His daughter answered that she did so out of necessity.

"I wasn't in touch very often because I knew you were thinking of having me kidnapped!" she shot back, also laughing—but not joking.

Later in the conversation, Mr. Gullery suggested that perhaps his father-in-law's view of the Unificationists is the prevalent one.

He said acquaintances often tell him "You seem like a decent, normal person, but I don't know about Reverend Moon."

ORGANIZATIONS TO CONTACT

The editors have compiled the following list of organizations concerned with the issues presented in this book. The descriptions are derived from materials provided by the organizations. All have publications or information available for interested readers. The list was compiled on the date of publication of the present volume; the information provided here may change. Be aware that many organizations take several weeks or longer to respond to inquiries, so allow as much time as possible.

American Family Foundation (AFF)
PO Box 2265, Bonita Springs, FL 34133
(941) 514-3081 • fax: (941) 514-3451
e-mail: aff@worldnet.att.net
website: http://www.csj.org

Founded in 1979, AFF is a secular research and educational organization that works to educate the public about cultic groups and psychological persuasion techniques. The foundation hosts workshops and programs to assist those who have been adversely affected by experiences with cults. In addition to a wide variety of books and other educational materials about cults, AFF publishes the *Cult Observer*, a monthly newsletter that tracks cultic activity around the world, and the *Cultic Studies Journal*, a scholarly research publication.

Center for Law and Religious Freedom (CLRF)
4208 Evergreen Ln., Suite 222, Annandale, VA 22003
(703) 642-1070 • fax: (703) 642-1075
e-mail: clrf@mindspring.com

The Center for Law and Religious Freedom was founded in 1975 to promote religious freedom. CLRF monitors cases affecting religious freedom and distributes information about legal issues involving religious exercise. The center publishes *Focus: On Justice, Reconciliation, and Religious Freedom*, which examines religious freedom issues, and the bimonthly periodical *Defender*.

Christian Research Institute (CRI)
PO Box 7000, Rancho Santa Margarita, CA 92688-7000
(949) 858-6100 • fax: (949) 858-6111
e-mail: p-young@ix.netcom.com
website: http://www.equip.org

The Christian Research Institute seeks to encourage orthodox, biblical Christianity. CRI disseminates information on cults, the occult, and other religious movements whose teachings and practices are inconsistent with the institute's biblical views. CRI broadcasts a daily, call-in radio program, *Bible Answer Man*, heard in Canada and the United States. The institute also publishes the *Christian Research Journal*, the *Christian Research Newsletter*, and numerous articles and books.

Cult Awareness Network (CAN)
117 South Cook St., Suite 354, Barrington, IL 60010
(773) 267-7777 • (800) 556-3055
e-mail: inform@cultawarenessnetwork.org
website: http://www.cultawarenessnetwork.org

CAN's primary goal is to promote religious freedom and the protection of religious and civil rights. CAN gathers information about diverse groups and religions, maintains an extensive reference database, and sponsors conferences open to the public. The network also staffs a national hotline for individuals who are concerned that their friends or relatives may be involved with a questionable religious group. CAN publishes a variety of educational brochures and booklets.

Family Action Information and Rescue (FAIR)
BCM Box 3535, PO Box 12
London WCIN 3XX
United Kingdom
44-1-539-3940

FAIR is a network of doctors, clergy, parents, ex-cultists, and others who seek to raise public awareness of unacceptable cult practices. The organization offers advice and support to individuals and distressed families who have been adversely affected by cult involvement. FAIR publishes a quarterly newsletter, as well as information and brochures on various cults.

International Cult Education Program (ICEP)
PO Box 1232, Gracie Station, New York, NY 10028
(212) 533-5420

Affiliated with the American Family Foundation, ICEP was established to educate staff and youth in high schools, universities, religious institutions, and other forums about the dangers of cults. ICEP provides educational materials that promote cult awareness and warn about the dangers of psychological manipulation.

International Religious Liberty Association (IRLA)
12501 Old Columbia Pike, Silver Spring, MD 20904
(301) 680-6680
e-mail: 74532.240@compuserve.com

IRLA is a multinational association that promotes universal freedom and respect for all religions, including minority religions. IRLA's publications include the bimonthly periodical *Liberty* and the semiannual *Conscience et Liberte*, which is published in English, French, German, Italian, Portuguese, and Spanish.

International Society for Krishna Consciousness (ISKCON)
3764 Watseka Blvd., Los Angeles, CA 90034
(800) 927-4152
website: http://www.harekrishna.com

The teachings and practices of the International Society for Krishna Consciousness are based in the Vedic scriptures of India. With thousands of followers worldwide, the movement maintains hundreds of temples in various cities. ISKCON publishes *Back to Godhead* magazine and *Hare Krishna World* and serves as a distributor of the spiritual literature of India.

Religious Movement Resource Center
629 South Howes, Fort Collins, CO 80521
(303) 490-2732
website: http://www.lamar.colostate.edu

The Religious Movement Resource Center specializes in cult research, offers counseling and support to those who have been adversely affected by cults, and runs a large network that investigates claims against specific cults. The center distributes research material, position papers, and film presentations designed to educate the public about cults.

Spiritual Counterfeits Project (SCP)
PO Box 4308, Berkeley, CA 94704
(510) 540-0300 • fax: (510) 540-1107
e-mail: scp@dnai.com
website: http://www.scp-inc.org

SCP is a Christian ministry that monitors spiritual trends, including cults, the occult, Eastern religions, and the New Age movement. The organization maintains an extensive library with files on cults and new religious movements and offers films, tapes, leaflets, outreach services, and counseling to the public. Its publications include the *SCP Newsletter* and the *SCP Journal,* as well as a variety of books and educational materials.

Watchman Fellowship
PO Box 530842, Birmingham, AL 35253
(205) 871-2858
e-mail: vantagewfi@aol.com
website: http://www.vantagewfi@aol.com

The Watchman Fellowship specializes in the study of new religious movements, including cults, the occult, and the New Age movement. The organization researches claims of questionable cult practices and provides counseling for former cult members. It offers film and slide presentations, audio tapes, books, and brochures, as well as publishing the *Watchman Expositor* magazine.

BIBLIOGRAPHY

Books

Harold Bloom	*The American Religion: The Emergence of the Post-Christian Nation.* New York: Simon & Schuster, 1992.
James J. Boyle	*Killer Cults.* New York: St. Martin's Press, 1995.
Daniel Cohen	*Cults.* Brookfield, CT: Millbrook Press, 1994.
Paul Keith Conkin	*American Originals: Homemade Varieties of Christianity.* Chapel Hill: University of North Carolina Press, 1997.
Arthur J. Deikman	*The Wrong Way Home: Uncovering the Patterns of Cult Behavior in American Society.* Boston: Beacon Press, 1994.
Kathlyn Gay	*Communes and Cults.* New York: Twenty-First Century Books, 1997.
David Christopher Lane	*Exposing Cults: When the Skeptical Mind Confronts the Mystical.* New York: Garland, 1994.
James R. Lewis, ed.	*From the Ashes: Making Sense of Waco.* Lanham, MD: Rowman and Littlefield, 1994.
James R. Lewis and J. Gordon Melton, eds.	*Church Universal and Triumphant in Scholarly Perspective.* Stanford, CA: Center for Academic Publications, 1994.
J. Gordon Melton	*The Encyclopedia of American Religions.* Detroit, MI: Gale Research, 1996.
J. Gordon Melton	*The Encyclopedic Handbook of Cults in America.* New York: Garland, 1992.
Susan Meredith	*Usborne Book of World Religions.* London: Usborne, 1995.
T. Miller, ed.	*America's Alternative Religions.* Albany, NY: SUNY Press, 1995.
Peter Occhiogrosso	*The Joy of Sects.* New York: Doubleday, 1996.
Loretta Orion	*Never Again the Burning Times: Paganism Revisited.* Prospect Heights, IL: Waveland Press, 1995.
Kay Marie Porterfield	*Straight Talk About Cults.* New York: Facts On File, 1995.
Anson Shupe and David Bromley, eds.	*Anti-Cult Movements in Cross-Cultural Perspective.* New York: Garland, 1994.
Thomas Streissguth	*Charismatic Cult Leaders.* Minneapolis, MN: Oliver Press, 1995.
Roger M. Thompson	*The Mormon Church.* New York: Hippocrene Books, 1993.
Stuart A. Wright, ed.	*Armageddon in Waco: Critical Perspectives on the Branch Davidian Conflict.* Chicago: University of Chicago Press, 1995.

Periodicals

Husayn Al-Kurdi — "Unsafe Sects," *Toward Freedom,* June/July 1998.

Jeannette Batz — "I Got Caught Up in a Cult," *Seventeen,* September 1995.

Fred Bayles and Patrick O'Driscoll — "Cybercults Earn Money, Recruit on Web," *USA Today,* March 28–30, 1997.

C. Bennett — "Killer Cults," *Fate,* July 1998. Available from 170 Future Way, Marion, OH 43305.

Thomas R. Casten — "Can We Prevent Cult Deaths?" *Skeptical Inquirer,* July/August 1997.

Loren Coleman — "Mysterious World," *Fate,* July 1997.

Rae Corelli — "Killer Cults," *Maclean's,* April 7, 1997.

Richard Corliss — "A Star Trek into the X-Files," *Time,* April 7, 1997.

Carolyn Gard — "The Power and Peril of Cults," *Current Health,* May 1997.

Issues and Controversies on File — "Cults," May 30, 1997. Available from Facts On File News Services, 11 Penn Plaza, New York, NY 10001-2006.

William F. Jasper — "Exposing the Web of Deceit," *New American,* September 1, 1997. Available from PO Box 8040, Appleton, WI 54913-9895.

David E. Kaplan and Andrew Marshall — "The Cult at the End of the World," *Wired,* July 1996. Available from 520 3rd St., Fourth Fl., San Francisco, CA 94107.

Dean Kelley — "Waco: A Massacre and Its Aftermath," *First Things,* May 1995. Available from Box 3000, Dept. FT, Denville, NJ 07834.

Cynthia Kisser — "The Road to Heaven's Gate," *Wall Street Journal,* April 1, 1997.

Lynne Lamberg — "Psychiatrist Explores Apocalyptic Violence in Heaven's Gate and Aum Shinrikyo Cults," *JAMA,* July 16, 1997. Available from the American Medical Association, Box 10945, Chicago, IL 60610.

Tanya Luhrmann — "Witches, Magic, Ordinary Folks: Why Entering a Cult Is Comforting and Feels a Lot Like Joining a Religion," *U.S. News & World Report,* April 7, 1997.

Martin E. Marty — "Playing with Fire: Looking at Heaven's Gate," *Christian Century,* April 16, 1997.

Kaylan Pickford — "I Lost My Daughter to a Cult," *Redbook,* March 1995.

Katha Pollitt — "Heaven Can Wait," *Nation,* April 28, 1997.

Charlie Reese — "Cults Spurn Conventional Religion," *Conservative Chronicle,* April 16, 1997. Available from PO Box 37077, Boone, Iowa 50037-0077.

Margaret O'Brien Steinfels — "Religion, True and False," *Commonweal,* April 25, 1997.

Margaret Talbot — "Married in a Mob," *New Republic,* December 22, 1997.

James Walsh — "Shoko Asahara: The Making of a Messiah," *Time,* April 3, 1995.

Leon Wieseltier — "Strait Was the Gate," *New Republic,* April 21, 1997.

INDEX

141